Empowering Generations

Blessing from God's Word

Kayla Grey

Text copyright © 2013 Kayla Grey. All rights reserved.

Published by Wisdom Press. Information contained within this book may not be copied, published, or otherwise shared without the author's express written consent.

Printed in the United States of America

ISBN 9-7806159400-7-6

Scripture taken from the New King James Version®. *Copyright © 1982 by Thomas Nelson, Inc. Used by permission.*

Name meanings have been utilized from James Strong, The Exhaustive Concordance of the Bible: Showing Every Word of the Text of the Common English Version of the Canonical Books, and Every Occurrence of Each Word in Regular Order., *electronic ed. (Ontario: Woodside Bible Fellowship., 1996).*

Book cover created by Core Spring Design (http://www.corespringdesign.com/).

- To my husband, Austin -
I love seeing your heart for family discipleship and teaching our kids about God's Word. From our many conversations, the book idea God gave me took root and has become Empowering Generations. *Thank you for encouraging me to keep on in the midst of an overwhelming task.*

- To my parents, Ben and Twilla -
The change God wrought in your marriage through the power of His blessing captivated me as a high school student. Now, as a wife and mom, I am grateful for all the Holy Spirit did in your lives to bring me to a point where this book was supernatural overflow.
To Him be the glory!

Contents

How to Use this Book

This book is not designed to detail every facet of each Bible figure's life. As such, I will highlight the anecdotes that line up with the theme/character trait emphasized. You will find the location of each person's stories noted at the beginning of each section for your ease and further study.

Throughout this book, I have utilized the New King James Version (NKJV). I find this to be an accurate "middle-ground" translation, especially between the KJV, ESV, and NIV. Feel free to look up the passages in your preferred translation. I include them within the text as a means of accurately summarizing the person being highlighted.

You will also notice that some "obscure" Bible figures are highlighted while some "famous" ones are missing. This is intentional. This book is merely meant to be a training ground for speaking the blessing into the lives of others. As such, I did not want to highlight all the "easy" people and leave you to sift through the lesser-known, nor did I want to give you only people you were less familiar with to show you how to do this. I aimed for balance. I hope that is obvious as you read through the summaries and blessings.

The summaries are written for you to read to yourself, though you may choose to read them to the person you are blessing if you deem it appropriate. The blessing at the end of each person's summary is intended to be read over the person you'd like to bless. The blessings are short to ease you into the concept of blessing and to help you become more comfortable with intentional times of blessing, but please add to them as the Holy Spirit leads! You know the person you want to bless, and the Spirit often gives specific words for that person at this point in his/her life.

I have also included creative ways to bless. While times of blessing are usually spoken, they don't always have to be. You may choose to create/write a blessing the person receiving can refer to again and again. At the end of the book, you will find a list of resources for further study on the concept of blessing – from YouTube videos to children's books, movies to music. I pray that this book would be the beginning of a legacy of blessing for you and your loved ones.

Death and life are in the power of the tongue, and those who love it will eat its fruit.

–Proverbs 18:21

There is power in the words we choose. Let's choose to use that power for the glory of God and the good of others.

I call heaven and earth as witnesses today against you, that I have set before you life and death, blessing and cursing; therefore choose life, that both you and your descendants may live; that you may love the LORD your God, that you may obey His voice, and that you may cling to Him, for He is your life and the length of your days…

-Deuteronomy 30:19-20a

What *is* a Blessing?

Thus says the Lord:

"Stand in the ways and see,
And ask for the old paths, where the good way is,
And walk in it;
Then you will find rest for your souls.
But they said, 'We will not walk in it.'"

-Jeremiah 6:16

We are often overcome by stress and shame simply because we have forsaken God's "old paths." Sure, many of us didn't intentionally forsake God's ways. In fact, most of us aren't even aware of the "ancient paths" referred to in Jeremiah 6:16 because we've grown up without them. We aren't Jewish, and it isn't part of our mode of operation.

It's time to go back. To seek His *olam nathiyb,* "ways from eternity past to eternity future," God's mode of operation. They aren't hard to find — when you are looking for them.

One of these ancient paths is that of blessing. We see it throughout Scripture – not only does God bless His people, but His people bless each other. In Hebrew, *barak* means "to bless," or – spiritually speaking – "to empower to prosper." The Greek word *eulogeo* means "to speak well of," the same spiritual connotation as *barak*.

Have you ever heard of the word *eulogy*? That word comes from the Greek word that means to bless! How sad it is that we usually speak eulogies at someone's funeral but rarely "speak well of" them while they are still living.

Many of us are floundering spiritually, emotionally, relationally, and financially because we have not received this "empowerment to prosper." That is the enemy's goal – to keep us from the riches of God and to convince us to settle for what is familiar. Are you comfortable with what you know? What if there's more that you're missing?

Prosperity can be success in: growing deeper in relationship with God, living "*peaceably with all men*" as Paul talks about in Romans 12:18, physical health, and – yes – even finances. Does this mean we should do "all the right things" so that God will give us health and wealth? No – that is not love; that's selfishness. God desires for us to be who **He** created us to be *for His glory,* and one of the ways we accomplish that is by affirming in others who God made *them* to be.

We see multiple examples of this in the Old Testament:

- Melchizedek blesses Abram. (Gen. 14:19-20)
- Isaac blesses Jacob. (Gen. 27:27-29)
- Jacob (Israel) blesses his 12 sons and two grandsons. (Gen. 48-49)
- David blesses Solomon. (1 Chron. 22:7-13)

And even in the New Testament:

- God the Father blesses Jesus, the Son. (Matt. 3:17)
- Jesus blesses Peter. (Matt. 16:17-19)
- Elizabeth blesses Mary. (Luke 1:42-45)
- Zacharias blesses John. (Luke 1:76-79)

These are only a few examples. As you pore through Scripture looking for examples of blessing, you will find them jump off the page. It becomes obvious that this, indeed, is one of God's forgotten ancient paths.

Why Bless?

Recently, I asked readers on my Facebook page if they had ever experienced a time of intentional, spoken blessing by their parents. One reader commented that she had. ***One.*** Out of the 50 people who saw the post, only one has received an intentionally spoken blessing. *Why?*

Our culture doesn't support it. This practice of speaking blessing was engrained in Jewish culture (by God's design!). It was and is not uncommon for the Shabbat meal (Sabbath) on Friday evenings to be followed by the father blessing his wife and each of his children. Can you imagine hearing every *week* growing up that God has awesome plans for your life, that He desires your obedience, that He delights in you?

We don't know it's missing. Because our culture doesn't support it, we don't even realize that God's desire for families to bless each other is absent. When I talk about "blessing someone," I am often met with blank stares or hesitant nods. It's not in our frame of reference, so it sounds incredibly foreign to us.

We don't know how. We're out of practice... and many of us don't know even where to start. Plus it could be awkward. Like learning how to ride a bicycle all over again -- except this time it's with real people and getting the kinks worked out could be uncomfortable at first.

We equate "positive" words with blessing, when they aren't always the same. While telling someone, "Good job!" is not cursing him/her, it's not the kind of blessing the Jews engaged in. The father didn't sit down and praise all the wonderful accomplishments his children had from the week. ***He spoke blessing over their identity (who they are), not their behavior (what they do).***

I think if we understood just how **crucial** blessing is in both the spiritual realm AND the physical realm, we would understand the urgency and importance of speaking those words over our children and those around us (parents, siblings, spouses, etc). The following is an excerpt quoted in *The Power of a Parent's Blessing*:

Max Jukes was an atheist who married a godless woman. Some 560 descendants were traced: 310 died as paupers, 150 became criminals, 7 of them murderers, 100 were known drunkards, and half the women were prostitutes. The descendants of Max Jukes cost the United States government more than 1.25 million dollars in 19th century dollars.

Jonathan Edwards was a contemporary of Max Jukes. He was a committed Christian who gave God first place in his life. He married a godly young lady, and some 1,394 descendants were traced: 295 graduated from college, of whom 13 became college presidents and 65 became professors, 3 were elected as United States senators, 3 as state governors and others were sent as ministers to foreign countries, 30 were judges, 100 were lawyers, one the dean of an outstanding law school, 56 practiced as physicians, one was the dean of a medical school, 75 became officers in the military, 100 were well-known missionaries, preachers and prominent authors, another 80 held some form of public office, of whom 3 were mayors of large cities, 1 was the comptroller of the U.S. Treasury, and another was the vice president of the United States. (p. 50-51)

[Clarification from Craig Hill: "This does not mean the family a person is born into determines his destiny... At any point it is possible to recognize and break the power of negative generational patterns and leave a godly heritage."]

Wow. Can you imagine a family legacy like Jonathan Edwards'? What an impact they have had on the United States. I believe we could see our own families thrive in the same way if we choose to return to God's ways -- one of which is blessing.

Who Should Bless?

Each person holds a variety of titles. While some may have a Ph.D. or MBA, some of us don't. Some of us have rather ordinary titles – son, daughter, brother, sister, husband, wife, dad, mom. These titles clue us in on important relationships in our lives. Such relationships are the very best place to begin blessing.

- Husbands, bless your wife. Wives, bless your husband.
- Parents, bless your child(ren).
- Brothers, bless your sisters. Sisters, bless your brothers.
- Aunts and uncles, bless your nieces and nephews.
- Grandparents, bless your grandchild(ren).
- Children, bless your parents.

It's not about creating the perfect blessing. It's about being intentional and affirming God's message of who he/she is and why he/she is here. Far too often, we allow the enemy to have access to our words. Let's begin being intentional about being God's mouthpiece instead.

Receiving the Father's Blessing

It is difficult to speak blessing over others when we have not received the blessing ourselves. God's design meant parents would be readily available to be His agents speaking blessing over children as they develop and grow. However, the enemy seeks access to impart his message -- one of worthlessness, devalue, and pain -- through parents whenever possible. ***Have you received God's message of who you are or Satan's?***

Unfortunately, most of us have heard Satan's message so often that we have accepted it as truth... but it's *not*. It's a lie, because he is the father of lies (John 8:44). Even a half-truth is a whole lie.

Please spend some time in God's Word and ask Him to reveal to you where you have believed the lies. He desperately longs for you to receive His truth about who you are... and to use you to impart His words of truth into the lives of others.

I am concluding this section with a ready-to-*accept* blessing. Before you continue reading this book, it is imperative that you receive God's blessing. A heart that is still believing lies, still seeking affirmation, still longing to be made whole is not a heart that will readily or easily speak blessing over others. These are words God wants to speak to **YOU**... His truth. He wanted you to know them a long time ago; will you receive them now?

If you have never received a name blessing, I would love to send you one! You can email me at renowncrowned@gmail.com. To God be the glory!

_______________, God rejoices over you.
Yes, **YOU**!! He rejoices over you (Zeph. 3:17). He is thrilled with who you are becoming. He is excited to commune with you. He delights in you.

He created you as His image-bearer. Even as His image-bearer, He has not left you alone in this life; He has given you His Spirit. You make mistakes. You say the wrong thing. You make a bad choice... But to your Father, ***these things do not define who you are***. He doesn't value you less when that word rolls off your tongue faster than you can stop it. He sees your worth separate from your actions. He sees His Son, who died to redeem you. When He considers Christ's sacrifice, He looks at you and says, "You are worth it."

Stop believing those lies that you're not good enough, pretty enough, strong enough. Stop listening to the enemy and pay attention to the One who created you. The One who calls you by name. The One who says, "You are Mine." (Is. 43:1)

How to Bless

Authors Dr. Gary Smalley and Dr. John Trent discuss five important components of Biblical blessing in their book, *The Blessing*: appropriate meaningful touch, a spoken message, attaching high value, picturing a special future, and a genuine commitment. Don't let that list overwhelm you, though. Blessing can be simple or ceremonial, frequent or at longer intervals (though I definitely recommend blessing intentionally more than once).

If you have a history of sarcasm, satire, or spite in your words, ask the Holy Spirit to reveal where you need to ask forgiveness from the person you wish to bless. Perhaps you made a passing comment in jest that the enemy used to implant his image into the person's heart – now would be an excellent time to ask God to show you what damage has been done and how it needs to be repaired.

Here are some ideas of what you could include in your blessing:

- Scripture! This is the ultimate Truth and blessing resource.

- Prayers you are praying
- Words of encouragement
- Affirmation of character qualities you have seen in the person's life
- Giving God glory for miracles performed in the person's life

Remember, the purpose of blessing is to affirm in someone who God has called him/her to be. Negative memories or traits should not be emphasized and ideally not mentioned unless good has come of those memories/traits. The blessings at the end of each section are a great starting point or model for you to see what you might say. Don't limit yourself (or God!) to the words on these pages. God is infinite, and there are many, many things He wants this person to know. What a privilege it is to be a conduit of God's message!

Creative Ways to Bless

Birthday Festivities – Make it a tradition! Include the opportunity for family and friends to speak words of blessing. If you have access to a voice recorder or camcorder, be sure to record it for listening/watching later.

Blessing Binder – Write letters, notes, poems, drawings, or collect special pictures at each birthday (maybe Christmas, too!). Compile it into a simple 3-ring binder using page protectors.

Blessing Prayer – If you write a letter of blessing, you may consider writing your blessing as a prayer to the LORD, thanking Him for various qualities and traits in the person you wish to bless that have blessed *you*.

Ceremony – Public blessing has a unique impact on the giver and receiver. This is a neat way to bless parents in old(er) age (See Craig Hill's *The Power of a Parent's Blessing*). It can also be a fabulous way to initiate a son/daughter into adulthood (See the movie Courageous).

Confetti Blessing – Make a list of things you are thankful for in the person you wish to bless (spouse, parents, child, coworker, etc). Then, cut out shapes (or use pre-cut shapes!) and write one item from the list on each shape. Tuck the shapes into an envelope and deliver (or mail) the confetti. What a fun way to see all the ways he/she has blessed you!

Framed Written Letter – Write a letter of blessing by hand and frame it. This can be an excellent Christmas, birthday, or anniversary gift – or anytime gift.

Full Body Blessing – This blessing is more intimate and better suited for a parent/child or spouse blessing. Go over each body part (general or specific), praying for the child or spouse in that area. Example: Head – *I pray Philippians 4:8– that whatever things are true, noble, just, pure, lovely, of good report – that you would think on these things.* Ears – *I pray that you would carefully filter what you hear from the media and absorb only what is Truth that lines up with God's Word.*

Love Letter Shower – SimplyRebekah.com talks about how she asked 71 of her husband's friends and family to write a blessing note ("love letter") and send it to her. She then gave him all 71 letters on his 30th birthday.

Name Acronym – Describe the person you wish to bless using the letters of their name. Example: SUE – Steadfast, Understanding, Encouraging; or JOHN – Just, Obedient, Helpful, Neat

Poetry – Blessings don't always have to be in prose. If you enjoy writing poetry, take the opportunity to bless someone with a poem especially about them.

Recorded Message – Using a camcorder or webcam, record your blessing message to the person you wish to bless. You can make the message as lengthy or as short as you'd like. Then either e-mail (if the file size is small enough), burn a DVD, or upload it to YouTube (you can put the settings on Private and send the person a special link to it). This is especially great for long distance blessing.

Get those creative juices flowing! You can use any of these ideas or come up with your own unique ideas. Just make sure the blessing happens!

Old Testament

Abel - Significance
Noah - Obedience
Abraham - Called
Joseph - Steward
Moses - Strengthened
Joshua - Trustworthy
Gideon - Valor
Samson - Set Apart
Boaz - Generous
Samuel - Success
David - Merciful
Elijah - Zealous
Micaiah - Steadfast
Josiah - Repentant
Solomon - Wisdom
Asa - Peace
Nehemiah - Boldness
Mordecai - Integrity
Daniel - Faithfulness

Abel – Significance
Meaning: Breath
Genesis 4:1-8

Now Adam knew Eve his wife, and she conceived and bore Cain, and said, "I have acquired a man from the Lord." Then she bore again, this time his brother Abel. Now Abel was a keeper of sheep, but Cain was a tiller of the ground. And in the process of time it came to pass that Cain brought an offering of the fruit of the ground to the Lord. Abel also brought of the firstborn of his flock and of their fat. And the Lord respected Abel and his offering, but He did not respect Cain and his offering. And Cain was very angry, and his countenance fell.

So the Lord said to Cain, "Why are you angry? And why has your countenance fallen? If you do well, will you not be accepted? And if you do not do well, sin lies at the door. And its desire is for you, but you should rule over it."

Now Cain talked with Abel his brother; and it came to pass, when they were in the field, that Cain rose up against Abel his brother and killed him.

-Genesis 4:1-8

There has been a lot of speculation over this anecdote from God's Word. Why did God receive Abel's offering but not Cain's? Perhaps

- God desired *firstfruits.*
- God wanted an *animal,* whose blood could be shed.
- Abel's heart *motivation* was pure and Cain's was not.

Hebrews gives us a glimpse:

By faith Abel offered to God a more excellent sacrifice than Cain, through which he obtained witness that he was righteous, God testifying of his gifts; and through it he being dead still speaks. (11:4)

We also know, from Hebrews 12:22-24, that Abel's sacrifice was a sign of what was to come.

But you have come ... to Jesus the Mediator of the new covenant, and to the blood of sprinkling that speaks better things than that of Abel.

God mentioned Abel briefly in comparison to the size of His Word, yet God doesn't waste words. He honored him by including him so that we could catch a glimpse of God's glory in Genesis 4.

Blessing of Abel

_________, today you may feel insignificant in the grand scheme of things. You may be wondering why God chose to place you on earth at this point in history. Why He placed you in the family He did. Why He gave you the color of eyes or hair He did. You may feel that you are of little value to a sovereign, holy God.

The truth, _________, is that He makes you significant through Christ. Abel is mentioned in a mere 10 verses in the entirety of Scripture, yet God chose to include him. I pray that you would be like Abel - that you would value obedient sacrifice to God above shortcuts. To obey is better than sacrifice (1 Sam. 15:22). That you would give Him your firstfruits rather than table scraps. That your faith in His providence would lead you to a solid trust in Him, even when it doesn't make sense.

You are valued and you are significant in God's sight. He placed you in this time for His glory. Seek Him above all else.

Noah – Obedience

Meaning: Rest

Genesis 6-9

This is the genealogy of Noah. Noah was a just man, perfect in his generations. Noah walked with God. And Noah begot three sons: Shem, Ham, and Japheth.

And God said to Noah, "The end of all flesh has come before Me, for the earth is filled with violence through them; and behold, I will destroy them with the earth. Make yourself an ark of gopherwood...everything that is on the earth shall die. But I will establish My covenant with you; and you shall go into the ark—you, your sons, your wife, and your sons' wives with you. And of every living thing of all flesh you shall bring two of every sort into the ark, to keep them alive with you; they shall be male and female.

Thus Noah did; according to all that God commanded him, so he did.

-Genesis 6:9-10, 13-19, 22

Not a peep. Scripture doesn't record any verbal response from Noah; simply "*thus Noah did."* *Why?* There are numerous characters in Scripture (and many of us!) who questioned God or at least verbalized some form of hesitancy. But no. God tells Noah there will be a flood so he needs to build a [huge] boat. Noah's response: He did "*according to all that God commanded him*" (even though it's quite possible Noah had no concept of rain or flooding).

It may have cost him a lot to do something so audacious. Friends, family, income... We can speculate what material consequences may have come from such faith and trust. But he did it.

In chapter 7, as God gathers the animals onto the ark, Scripture again notes:

And Noah did according to all that the Lord commanded him. (7:5)

It was worth it though. We know that from verse 23 of chapter 7:

So He destroyed all living things which were on the face of the ground: both man and cattle, creeping thing and bird of the air. They were destroyed from the earth. Only Noah and those who were with him in the ark remained alive.

After the floodwaters subsided, Noah built an altar to the LORD and offered sacrifices. God blessed Noah and his sons with the privilege and commission to "*Be fruitful and multiply, and fill the earth*" (9:1). He also established a covenant with Noah, Noah's sons, and every living creature:

Thus I establish My covenant with you: Never again shall all flesh be cut off by the waters of the flood; never again shall there be a flood to destroy the earth. (9:11)

After this, God gave the rainbow as the sign of His covenant. Not only was Noah's obedience rewarded with preservation of his life, the privilege of "being fruitful and multiplying" after the flood, and entering covenant with the One True God, but he also received a visual reminder of God's covenant - one that *we*, generations removed from Noah, have the privilege to see and remember God's covenant.

Noah's obedience cost him everything, but he also had a whole lot to gain. If he had chosen not to obey, the story would've ended quite differently.

Blessing of Noah

_________, if you seek God, you will find Him when you search for Him with all your heart (Jer. 29:13). When you seek Him, He transforms your mind (Rom. 8:1-2) and desires (Ps. 37:4). You will often find great joy in following Christ, but the enemy wants to rob you of this joy (John 10:10).

I pray that you, _________, would be obedient to God like Noah. Genesis says, "Noah did according to all that the Lord commanded him." There is no record of his hesitation or questioning God; what we *do* know is that he was obedient. Obedience for him was ***hard*** - Hebrew tells us, "By faith Noah, being divinely warned of things not yet seen, moved with godly fear, prepared an ark for the saving of his household, by which he condemned the world and became heir of the righteousness which is according to faith." (Heb. 11:7) It wasn't easy to be different and follow God, but it was worth it!

As you trust the LORD and walk in obedience, keep your eyes fixed on Jesus. He will never leave you nor forsake you (Deut. 31:6b).

Abraham – Called

Meaning: Father of a Multitude

Genesis 11-17

The trek out of familiarity began with Terah in Genesis 11. He took his son (Abram), his daughter-in-law (Sarai), and grandson (Lot, son of Haran), and *"they went out with them from Ur of the Chaldeans to go to the land of Canaan; and they came to Haran and dwelt there"* (11:31). Terah died in Haran (11:32), but why did he even leave in the first place? Scripture doesn't say.

When Abram was 75 years old, he left Haran. Sarai, Lot, and all their possessions and servants went with him (12:4-5). Scripture <u>does</u> tell us why Abram left the semi-familiarity of Haran for a place called Canaan. The LORD had spoken this to Abram:

Get out of your country, from your family and from your father's house, to a land that I will show you. I will make you a great nation; I will bless you and make your name great; and you shall be a blessing. I will bless those who bless you, and I will curse him who curses you; and in you all the families of the earth shall be blessed. (12:1-3)

And thus they left. When they arrived, the LORD again visited Abram and reminded him, *"To your descendants I will give this land"* (12:7). Famine struck the land though, so the entourage ended up in Egypt. After the famine was over, they returned to Canaan.

Abram had gained much livestock, silver, and gold while they lived in Egypt (see Gen. 12:10-20), but when Abram, Sarai, and Lot returned to Canaan, *"the land was not able to support them, that they might dwell together, for their possessions were so great that they could not dwell together"* (13:6). Abram asked Lot to choose where he'd like to live – Abram and Sarai would live wherever Lot did not choose. Lot went east, and Abram stayed put. (13:10-13)

Two chapters later, we see the LORD entered covenant with Abram. The LORD promised not only one son to this childless man, but descendants as numerous as the stars (15:5). *"And he believed in the LORD, and He accounted it to him for righteousness"* (15:6).

At the ripe old age of ninety-nine, the LORD appeared again to Abram. Abram's wife,

Sarai, still had not borne a son. Where would this heir come from? Abram fell on his face in a combination of fear and worship. God talked to him, saying:

As for Me, behold, My covenant is with you, and you shall be a father of many nations. No longer shall your name be called Abram, but your name shall be Abraham; for I have made you a father of many nations. (17:5)

His original promise had increased. Not only would the LORD make Abra(ha)m a great nation, but now also He promised to make him the father of **many** nations!

I will make you exceedingly fruitful; and I will make nations come from you. And I will establish My covenant between Me and you and your descendants after you. Also I give to you and your descendants after you the land in which you are a stranger, all the land of Canaan, as an everlasting possession; and I will be their God. (17:6-8)

Can you imagine if Abram had stayed in Haran? How that would have changed the course of history! Instead, when God called,

Abram answered with obedience. And through his Seed, all nations have been blessed.

Blessing of Abraham

_________, He who has called you is faithful. The LORD chose you to bring Him glory and to shine His light before others so that they, too, could learn of and respond to His calling.

I pray for you, _________, that you would answer the LORD's call, just as Abraham did. He left a land that was familiar on a quest for what was promised. He entered covenant with God. He believed God and it was "accounted to him as righteousness." Abraham wasn't perfect, but he was willing. He wasn't always wise, but he trusted God to fulfill His promise. Long after Abraham's death, God fulfilled His promise to Abraham. All nations have been blessed through the sacrifice of Christ on the cross for our sins; He is the Seed of Abraham.

"But you are a chosen generation, a royal priesthood, a holy nation, His own special people, that you may proclaim the praises of Him who called you out of darkness into His marvelous light; who once were not a people but are now the people of God, who had not obtained mercy but now have obtained mercy" (1 Pet. 2:9-10). May your life exude the riches of His calling.

Joseph – Steward

Meaning: Jehovah has Added

Genesis 37-45

Joseph's life begins as the fulfillment of his mother Rachel's deep-seated desire to bear a son for her husband Jacob. Joseph was Jacob's favorite (Gen. 37:3), so when Joseph received a dream and told his brothers, God's Word says, "*and they hated him even more*" (37:5). Two dreams – one of sheaves in a field and another of the sun, moon, and stars – placed Joseph in a place of honor while the others were bowing before him. As a result, his brothers "*conspired against him to kill him*" (37:18). Rather than killing him, they decided to sell him as a slave to traders headed to Egypt.

In Egypt, he was purchased by Potiphar, the captain of the guard (39:1).

The LORD was with Joseph, and he was a successful man; and he was in the house of his master the Egyptian…So Joseph found favor in his sight, and served him. (39:2, 4)

Joseph became the overseer of Potiphar's house, to the point where Potiphar "*left all that he had in Joseph's hand"* (39:6). Potiphar's wife, though, attempted to seduce him. When he refused, she called the men and accused Joseph of seducing her – and when Potiphar heard this, he put Joseph in prison (39:20).

Yet again, Joseph was granted favor.

The keeper of the prison committed to Joseph's hand all the prisoners who were in the prison; whatever they did there, it was his doing. The keeper of the prison did not look into anything that was under Joseph's authority, because the LORD was with him; and whatever he did, the LORD made it prosper. (39:22-23)

While in prison, Joseph interpreted two dreams for fellow prisoners, requesting that one mention him upon release (40:14). The prisoner failed (40:23), and two years later, Pharaoh dreamed a dream. The former prisoner remembered Joseph and recommended him when all others were unable to interpret Pharaoh's dream (41:9-13). When brought before Pharaoh, Joseph gave glory where it is due:

It is not in me; God will give Pharaoh an answer of peace. (41:16)

And then he interpreted it. Pharaoh honored Joseph by putting him second-in-command of all Egypt (41:40-41). Part of Pharaoh's dream had been a warning of a coming famine, which Joseph helped prepare for by stockpiling grain during the good years.

When the famine came, it impacted every nation except Egypt. Word quickly passed that Egypt had grain, so many people purchased grain from Egypt – including Joseph's brothers (42:7). When they entered Joseph's presence, they didn't recognize him; but Joseph recognized them (42:8). He sent them back to Canaan to bring their youngest brother, Benjamin, to see him. After much pleading with Jacob, the brothers returned to Egypt. Joseph set up a variety of encounters with the brothers but finally revealed himself to them. His words are astonishing:

I am Joseph your brother, whom you sold into Egypt. But now, do not therefore be grieved or angry with yourselves because you sold me here; for God sent me before you to preserve life. For these two years the famine has been in the land, and there are still five years in which there will be neither plowing nor harvesting. And God sent me before you to preserve a posterity for you in the earth, and to save your lives by a great deliverance. So now it was not you who sent me here, but God; and He has made me a father to Pharaoh, and lord of all his house, and a ruler throughout all the land of Egypt. (45:4-8)

He encouraged his brothers to go back to their father and then return to Egypt, where Joseph would provide pastureland for them. Even after all he had been through, Joseph still looked for the positive, the providence of God, in his circumstances. And he glorified Him.

Blessing of Joseph

__________, it is amazing to see how God has worked and is continuing to work in your life. He has a great plan for your life, one that is for your good and His glory. What a privilege it is to be made a worthy vessel to honor and glorify the Sovereign Lord.

I pray for you, __________, that you would seek to honor God, whatever your circumstance, like Joseph did. He didn't give up on God, and he didn't praise Him only when things were going well. His wisdom and management skills did not go unnoticed by the leaders of Egypt; they wanted his direction and guidance, and it was obvious to them that he was not doing it in his own strength. I pray you will desire to operate in God's power and make the most of every opportunity you are provided.

May your responsibilities be a testimony of the goodness of God in your life, and may God grant you wisdom in knowing how to handle those responsibilities. Praise the LORD for His guiding hand.

Moses – Strengthened

Meaning: Drawn [out of the water]

Exodus 2-4

Born during a time when all the Hebrew males were to be killed, Moses' parents must have known that God had big things in store for their son. They could only hide him about three months (Ex. 2:2), after which time his mother placed him in *"an ark of bulrushes"* and laid him in the reeds by the river bank (2:3). Pharaoh's daughter discovered him, called for a nurse (who was actually Moses' mother!), and brought him up as her own son (4:8-10).

As an adult, Moses fled the feared consequences of his actions (4:11-15) and arrived in Midian. He took a wife and became the shepherd of his father-in-law's flock. As his was doing this task, *"the Angel of the LORD appeared to him in a flame of fire from the midst of the bush. So he looked, and behold the bush was burning with fire, but the bush was not consumed."* (3:2)

Finding this an odd sight, Moses stopped to check it out. God calls to him from the bush,

"Moses! Moses!" To which Moses replied, *"Here I am."*

The LORD told Moses of the cries of the Israelites, that He desired to deliver them and bring them to the Promised Land, and that He has chosen Moses for the task (3:5-10). Moses wasn't so sure that was a great idea:

"Who am I that I should go to Pharaoh, and that I should bring the children of Israel out of Egypt?"

God, however, knew exactly what He was doing:

"I will certainly be with you. And this shall be a sign to you that I have sent you: When you have brought the people out of Egypt, you shall serve God on this mountain."

Moses knew how unbelievable this task will be to the Israelites. He told God he needs more information. What should he tell them if they ask who sent him?

"I AM WHO I AM…Thus you shall say to the children of Israel, 'I AM has sent me to you'…Thus you shall say to the children of Israel: 'The LORD God of your fathers, the God of Abraham, the God of Isaac, and the God of Jacob, has sent me to you. This is

My name forever, and this is My memorial to all generations'..." (3:14-15)

God charged Moses with the task of appearing before Pharaoh and requesting the release of the Israelites. Moses still wasn't sure they would believe, so God performed a couple of miracles (Moses' rod became a snake and then returned to a rod, and Moses' hand became leprous and then was restored, 4:1-7) to reassure Moses of His sovereignty and involvement in the situation; after all, it's for His glory anyway. These were signs Moses could use to show his audience the LORD was, indeed, using him. After a bit more debate about Moses' hesitancies and even the anger of the LORD kindling against Moses (4:8-17), Moses went (4:20).

He encountered Pharaoh 11 times (Ex. 5-12). Moses led the Israelites out of captivity, strengthened by the mighty hand of God to do so.

Blessing of Moses

__________, you were created to honor God – in your words and your actions. It is no small task to be commissioned by the God of the universe to seek Him and then lead others to Him. What an awesome privilege.

I pray for you, __________, that you would not seek to do things in your own strength, but fully rely on God as Moses did. Moses hesitated; he knew his own inadequacies very well, and he reminded God of these when God called him to the very important task of delivering Israel from the hand of Pharaoh. Over and over, God promised to be with him and to give him the right words. Finally, Moses obeyed and went. God's power was sufficient for the task He called Moses to.

May you not hesitate to rely fully upon His strength, even when you think you can do it alone. May your strength be rooted in the One who is all-powerful. And may your life be a vibrant testimony of the power of God for salvation for all who believe (Rom. 1:16).

Joshua – Trustworthy
Meaning: Jehovah is Salvation
Numbers 13-14

We first meet Moses' assistant, Joshua, in Exodus 17, where Moses instructs him to choose some men and fight Amalek. Joshua led these men to defeat Amalek and his people (17:13). The LORD was with him.

In Numbers 13, Moses sends a male from each of the tribes of Israel to spy out the land of Canaan, including Joshua (from the tribe of Ephraim). After forty days of spying out the land, the men returned to the Israelites. Caleb, from the tribe of Judah, suggested, *"Let us go up at once and take possession, for we are well able to overcome it"* (13:30). The other men were not so convinced. *"And they gave the children of Israel a bad report of the land which they had spied out, saying, 'The land…is a land that devours its inhabitants, and all the people whom we saw in it are men of great stature…and we were like grasshoppers in our own sight, and so we were in their sight."* (13:32-33)

Of course, the Israelites had no desire to enter such a daunting place; it didn't matter to them that this was the land God had promised them. They desired to return to the "comforts" of Egypt and even proposed selecting a leader and going back (14:2-4)! Joshua and Caleb "*tore their clothes; and they spoke to all the congregation of the children of Israel, saying: 'The land we passed through to spy out is an exceedingly good land. If the LORD delights in us, then He will bring us into this land and give it to us, "a land which flows with milk and honey." Only do not rebel against the LORD, nor fear the people of the land, for they are our bread; their protection has departed from them, and the LORD is with us. Do not fear them.'*" (14:6-9)

The LORD then spoke to Moses about Israel's rejection of Him. As their interaction concluded, He said to both Moses and Aaron, "*Say to them, 'As I live,' says the LORD, 'just as you have spoken in My hearing, so I will do to you: The carcasses of you who have complained against Me shall fall in this wilderness…Except for Caleb, the son of Jephunneh and Joshua the son of Nun, you shall by no means enter the land which I swore I would make you dwell in"* (14:28-30). Why did God make such an exception for Caleb and Joshua? They stood on His promise, trusted Him, and encouraged the people to do likewise – even when it was unpopular to do so. They proved themselves to be trustworthy.

Joshua became Moses' successor in leading the Israelites (Num. 27:18-22, Deut. 31:3). As Moses passed the baton to Joshua, he spoke this blessing over him *"in the sight of all Israel"*:

Be strong and of good courage, for you must go with this people to the land which the LORD has sworn to their fathers to give them, and you shall cause them to inherit it. And the LORD, He is the One who goes before you. He will be with you, He will not leave you nor forsake you; do not fear nor be dismayed. (Deut. 31:7-8)

These words were planted in the mind of Joshua by his predecessor… So it's not surprising that after Moses died, the LORD spoke to Joshua and said this:

…No man shall be able to stand before you all the days of your life; as I was with Moses, so I will be with you. I will not leave you nor forsake you. Be

strong and of good courage, for to this people you shall divide as an inheritance the land which I swore to their fathers to give them. Only be strong and very courageous, that you may observe to do according to all the law which Moses My servant commanded you…Have I not commanded you? Be strong and of good courage; do not be afraid, nor be dismayed, for the LORD your God is with you wherever you go. (Josh. 1:5-7, 9)

Blessing of Joshua

__________, God's Word is truth. It is the plumb line, the source we have to compare all other information against. It is sufficient for salvation and inerrant for study. Through it, God calls us to be in the world and not of it (Rom. 2:2).

I pray for you, __________, that you would be trustworthy just as Joshua was. He was given great responsibility when Moses sent him with other leaders to search out the land of Canaan. That responsibility was tested upon his return. It would have been easy to join the others who were complaining about the giants that lived in Canaan, or even to just say nothing. Instead, he and Caleb stood firm on God's promise to give Israel the land. They used their words to point others back to what God had promised, even when their audience wasn't listening. And God didn't overlook their faithfulness in speaking the truth. He blessed them with life, while the others who complained did not inherit the Promised Land.

May your words and actions affirm to those around you that God is with you. May it be obvious that God still keeps His promises. May you never hesitate to speak truth, especially in the midst of easy-to-believe lies.

Gideon – Valor

Meaning: Hewer [one who chops down]

Judges 6-8

From the very first interaction between the Angel of the LORD and Gideon, the Angel called out greatness in him:

"The LORD is with you, you mighty man of valor!" (Judges 6:12)

Gideon questioned why the Midianites had overtaken Israel; isn't God a God of miracles? The LORD then gave Gideon a seemingly impossible task:

"Go in this might of yours, and you shall save Israel from the hand of the Midianites. Have I not sent you?" (6:14)

Gideon hesitated. He's a "nobody" among the tribes of Israel:

"O my Lord, how can I save Israel? Indeed my clan is the weakest in Manasseh, and I am the least in my father's house." (6:15)

Even after the LORD again affirmed that Gideon would be the one to defeat the Midianites (in the strength of the LORD), Gideon asked for a sign. He needed assurance. Gideon prepared goat meat, bread, and broth and presented it to the Angel. Gideon received his sign:

Then the Angel of the LORD put out the end of the staff that was in His hand, and touched the meat and the unleavened bread; and fire rose out of the rock and consumed the meat and the unleavened bread. And the Angel of the LORD departed out of his sight. (6:21)

It occurred to Gideon that he had, indeed, seen the Angel of the LORD face to face, so the LORD replied to his fear: "*Peace be with you; do not fear, you shall not die.*" (6:23)

The LORD commissioned Gideon to take one of his father's bulls, tear down the altar to Baal, and build an altar to the LORD, where he could offer the bull as a burnt sacrifice. Scripture notes that Gideon was afraid of his father's house, so he did so by night. The next day, Gideon's father Joash was told by the men of the city that Gideon should die for what he'd done. Joash replied that if Baal really is a god, he should be able to plead for himself. [The people then called Gideon "Jerubbaal," which means contender with Baal.]

The Midianites then joined forces with the Amalekites. *"But the Spirit of the LORD came upon Gideon…"* (6:34). Even so, Gideon again needed assurance. He placed a fleece on the threshing floor and asked God to keep the ground dry but the fleece wet with dew. God did so. The next day, Gideon requested the opposite – dry fleece and wet ground; again, God did so.

Gideon had gathered quite an army to take on the Midianites, but the LORD told him to thin out the ranks. Why? *"lest Israel claim glory for itself against Me, saying 'My own hand has saved me'"* (7:2). Through various means, the army Gideon leads shrank from 33,000 to 300. After some pursuit, *"thus Midian was subdued before the children of Israel, so that they lifted their heads no more. And the country was quiet for 40 years in the days of Gideon."* (8:28)

Blessing of Gideon

__________, God chose to place your life at this time in history for a reason. He knows what opportunities you will face and what trials you will go through, but He did not put you in the wrong era of history. He wants you to impact this world for His glory NOW.

I pray for you, __________, that you would be a mighty man/woman of valor – not in your own might, but as Gideon was – in the strength of the LORD. Gideon did some hard things, like tearing down the altar to Baal and fighting the Midianites with an insanely small army (ridiculed by some of his countrymen). He also had awesome privilege – he saw the Angel of the LORD face to face and was made great in the midst of his inadequacies. I pray you would allow the LORD to use you in any way He sees fit – for the hard things and the awesome privileges.

May your identity be rooted in Christ, not your earthly accomplishments or failures. Gideon was valued by God before he did any "great things" for Him. Your worth is not in what you do but in who you are.

Samson – Set Apart
Meaning: Like the Sun
Judges 13-15

The Angel of the LORD visited the barren wife of a man named Manoah; He promised a son. This son *"shall be a Nazirite to God from the womb,"* which meant he must keep to strict dietary habits and not shave his head – he must be set apart from those around him. Yet he would *"begin to deliver Israel out of the hand of the Philistines"* (13:5). She went and told her husband, who responded by praying, *"O my Lord, please let the Man of God whom You sent come to use again and teach us what we shall do for the child who will be born."* (13:8)

What faith! The Angel of the LORD visited them again, reminding them of what He had told her the first time (13:13-14). When Manoah and his wife offered the Angel of the LORD food, He declined and requested that they offer a burnt offering to the LORD instead. They did just this, and *"as the flame went up toward heaven from the altar—the Angel of the LORD ascended in the flame of the altar!"* (13:20)

Manoah panicked, saying that because they have seen God, they shall surely die. His wife responded differently:

"If the LORD had desired to kill us, He would not have accepted a burnt offering and a grain offering from our hands, nor would He have shown us all these things, nor would He have told us such things as these at this time."

Later in Samson's life, he pursued a relationship with a Philistine woman. As he traveled to her, he encountered a young lion. *"And the Spirit of the LORD came mightily upon him, and he tore the lion apart as one would have torn apart a young goat, though he had nothing in his hand…"* (14:6a)

After they married, Samson presented a riddle to a group of Philistine men, saying the whoever lost would owe the other party 30 linen garments and 30 changes of clothing. They were stumped for 7 days and asked Samson's wife to find out the answer. Seven days later, Samson finally relented and told her the answer. She passed the answer on to the men, and Samson became furious:

"Then the Spirit of the LORD came upon him mightily, and he went down to Ashkelon and killed thirty of their men, took their apparel, and gave the changes of clothing to those who had explained the riddle…" (14:19)

Samson returned to his wife, but *"her father would not permit him to go in"* (15:1). He had given her to Samson's companion. Samson responded: *"'This time I shall be blameless regarding the Philistines if I harm them!' Then Samson went and caught three hundred foxes; and he took torches, turned the foxes tail to tail, and put a torch between each pair of tails. When he had set the torches on fire, he let the foxes go into the standing grain of the Philistines, and burned up both the shocks and the standing grain, as well as the vineyards and olive groves."* (15:3-5)

In retaliation, the Philistines burned Samson's former wife and her father. Samson hid in the rock of Etam, where the men of Judah found and arrested him to turn him over to the Philistines. After being bound, *"Then the Spirit of the LORD came mightily upon him; and the ropes that were on his arms became like flax that is burned with fire and his bonds broke loose from his hands. He found a fresh jawbone of a donkey, reached out his hand and took it, and killed a thousand men with it."* (15:14-15)

Obviously set apart and led by the Spirit of the LORD, Samson did mighty deeds. He was the fulfillment of a promise the Angel of the LORD had brought to his father and mother in barrenness. He wasn't without faults, but the LORD still used him in awesome ways.

Blessing of Samson

_________, you were chosen by God to live at this time in history to glorify Him and lead others to Christ. He has created you in His image, with emotions and intellect to enable you to engage those around you. God planned for you to be here now!

I pray for you, _________, that your life would be a set apart and led by the Spirit, just as Samson's was. His mother refrained from wine and anything unclean while she was pregnant with Samson because God had instructed her to do so. Samson was a mighty force for the LORD when the Spirit stirred him to action. I pray that you would not hesitate to act when the Spirit moves in your heart! Follow His leading.

May you be set apart from those around you. May they see in you the light of Christ and glorify God, and may you experience life to the fullest as you live in His power.

Boaz – Generous

Meaning: Fleetness

Ruth 2-4

A widow returned to her homeland of Israel, along with her Moabite widowed daughter-in-law. With no human as their source of provision, Ruth asked Naomi to allow her to follow the custom of the land – to go out and glean from the corners of the field whatever the workers have left behind. (Lev. 23:22, Deut. 24:21)

Ruth went and gleaned, happening upon Boaz's part of the field (Ruth 2:3). Boaz saw this from a distance and called together his reapers. He asked who the young woman is, and the head servant informed him. *"It is the young Moabite woman who came back with Naomi from the country of Moab. And she said, 'Please let me glean and gather after the reapers among the sheaves.' So she came and has continued from morning until now, though she rested a little in the house."* (2:6-7)

Boaz went to Ruth and told her to not glean from any other field but to follow his workers. He also said, *"Have I not commanded the young men not to touch you? And when you are thirsty, go to the vessels and drink what the young men have drawn."* (2:9)

Ruth was humbled by this generosity. She was merely a foreigner (2:10); why was she anything special? Boaz responded:

"It has been fully reported to me, all that you have done for your mother-in-law since the death of your husband, and how you have left your father and your mother and the land of your birth, and have come to a people whom you did not know before. The LORD repay your work, and a full reward by given you by the LORD God of Israel, under whose wings you have come for refuge." (2:11-12)

Ruth's character preceded her. Boaz knew she had no one to provide for her, so he stepped up and provided for her generously. He went so far as to tell his reapers, *"Let her glean even among the sheaves, and do not reproach her. Also let grain from the bundles fall purposely for her; leave it that she may glean, and do not rebuke her."* (2:15b-16)

Some time later, at the encouragement of Naomi, Ruth presented herself to Boaz in a potentially compromising situation and requested that he *"take your maidservant* [Ruth] *under your wing, for you are a close relative"* (3:9b). Boaz was related to Naomi's late husband, Elimelech, and custom was that widows could be "redeemed" by another male family member (married to him) to continue the legacy of the deceased. This is what Ruth requested. (Deut. 25:5-10)

Boaz replied, "*…And now, my daughter, do not fear. I will do for you all that you request, for all the people of my town know that you are a virtuous woman. Now it is true that I am a close relative; however, there is a relative closer than I. Stay this night, and in the morning it shall be that if he will perform the duty of a close relative for you – good; let him do it. But if he does not want to perform the duty for you, then I will perform the duty for you, as the LORD lives!..."* (3:11-13)

Was this required of him? No. He could have directed Ruth to the "closer relative" rather than taking the time and effort to do so himself. Yet he found this worth his time and effort. The closer relative did not want to jeopardize his own inheritance, so Boaz was able to redeem Ruth and take her as his wife. (4:1-11)

In the grand scheme of things, did his generosity go unnoticed? Not at all. Matthew 1 and Luke 3 recount the genealogy of Christ…Boaz is named in both. Not only was he the great-grandfather of King David, he was a part of the family line from which the Messiah came!

Blessing of Boaz

__________, when God created you, He created someone to bear His image. You have intrinsic value because the Creator placed that value in your personhood before you were even born. He wants you to make choices that honor and glorify Him. He desires for you to be an excellent image-bearer.

I pray for you, __________that you would have a spirit of generosity just as Boaz had. He did not cut corners or give the bare minimum; he went above and beyond. He saw a need and met it intentionally. Boaz could have easily seen it as an unnecessary burden and Ruth as annoying. Not so – he delighted to bless Ruth and Naomi, both verbally and through physical provision (grain).

May the LORD place in your heart a desire to give, not merely receive. May you willingly go out of your way to care for those around you who have no one else to turn to. Let your light shine before men that they may see your good works and glorify your Father in heaven. (Matt. 5:16)

Samuel – Success

Meaning: His name is El

1 Samuel 2-3, 7

The son Hannah so longed for was finally granted to her, and she dedicated him to temple service – just as she had vowed she would (1 Samuel 1:11, 24-28). We are told Samuel ministered before the LORD, *"even as a child"* (2:18). Hannah was blessed with three more sons and two daughters, and *"the child Samuel grew before the LORD."* (2:21)

The first time the LORD called to Samuel, he did not recognize His voice and ran to Eli instead (3:4-5). The LORD called a second time, and Samuel again went to Eli (3:6). Scripture tells us, *"Now Samuel did not yet know the LORD, nor was the word of the LORD yet revealed to him"* (3:7). It makes sense, then, that Samuel would seek out the person most familiar to him – Eli. A third time the LORD called, and Samuel went to Eli. Eli realized what was happening and instructed Samuel to wait and, if the LORD called again, to respond, *"Speak, LORD, for Your servant hears."* (3:9)

The LORD called Samuel, and he responded, *"Speak, for Your servant hears"* (3:10). With this, the LORD gave Samuel his first prophecy, related to Eli's household. The next morning, Eli asked what the LORD had said, and Samuel *"told him everything, and hid nothing from him."* (3:17-18)

So Samuel grew, and the LORD was with him and let none of his words fall to the ground (3:19). His credibility was established, as the next verse tells us: *"And all Israel from Dan to Beersheba knew that Samuel had been established as a prophet of the LORD."* Of course, the test of a true prophet or false prophet was whether or not his words came to pass (Deut 18:21-22). So the LORD granted Samuel success from the beginning of his time as prophet of Israel.

Many years later, Samuel spoke to Israel, saying, *"If you return to the LORD with all your hearts, then put away the foreign gods and the Ashtoreths from among you, and prepare your hearts for the LORD, and serve Him only; and He will deliver you from the hand of the Philistines." So the children of Israel put away the Baals and the*

Ashtoreths, and served the LORD only (1 Sam. 7:3-4). Success again.

Samuel called for a gathering at Mizpah, and while the Israelites were there, they *"fasted that day, and said there, 'We have sinned against the LORD'"* (7:5-6). The Philistines found out about Israel meeting at Mizpah and planned an attack. When the Israelites found out about it, they pleaded with Samuel to *"cry out to the LORD our God for us, that He may save us from the hand of the Philistines"* (7:8). Samuel did just that. He offered a lamb as a burnt offering and cried out to the LORD on Israel's behalf. The LORD answered him (7:9).

Now as Samuel was offering up the burnt offering, the Philistines drew near to battle against Israel. But the LORD thundered with a loud thunder upon the Philistines that day, and so confused them that they were overcome before Israel. And the men of Israel went out of Mizpah and pursued the Philistines, and drove them back as far as below Beth Car. Then Samuel took a stone and set it up between Mizpah and Shen, and called its name Ebenezer, saying, "Thus far the LORD has helped us."

So the Philistines were subdued, and they did not come anymore into the territory of Israel. And the hand of the LORD was against the Philistines all the days of Samuel. Then the cities which the Philistines had taken from Israel were restored to Israel…And Samuel judged Israel all the days of his life. (7:10-14)

The LORD showed Himself to be mighty through one man in Israel at this time. The LORD granted Samuel success in his role as prophet and judge of Israel. The LORD granted Israel success through Samuel's leadership.

Blessing of Samuel

_________, the world has told us to pursue success at all costs. Typically this means financial success or fame. However, God's Word and His ways stand in stark contrast to the world system. Does He condemn success? No. But it must be considered in balance, not extremes.

I pray for you, _________, that you would receive the success the LORD grants you, as Samuel did. He served the LORD from the time he was a child, and when it came time for him to hear God's Word to Israel, he was eager to listen. The LORD verified Samuel's message by fulfilling that which He had spoken to him (and then Samuel spoke to Israel). The LORD also gave Israel victory over the Philistines while Samuel led Israel. Israel regained territory they had lost and "the hand of the LORD was against the Philistines all the days of Samuel." (1 Sam. 7:13) Samuel was granted success in leadership and prophecy because it testified to God's might on Israel's behalf.

Success, in its most basic form, forces us to choose who we will glorify – ourselves or the LORD. Sometimes the LORD grants financial success and influence but not always. Regardless, He calls us to faithfulness in serving Him (rather than ourselves), and He will do the rest.

David – Merciful

Meaning: Beloved

1 Samuel 18-2 Samuel 9

We meet David first in 1 Samuel 16, when the prophet Samuel anoints him king over Israel. This would typically be time for a grand celebration… except that Saul was still king, and he was not ready to give up his authority. So David waited for a time before he could assume the throne.

In the meantime, David played his harp to soothe Saul, who was troubled by a distressing spirit (16:14-23), and conquered the giant Philistine, Goliath (1 Sam. 17). Yet Saul was anything but pleased with David. After David's victory, *"the women sang as they danced, and said: 'Saul has slain his thousands, and David his ten thousands'"* (18:7). This was too much for Saul; he *"was very angry, and the saying displeased him…So Saul eyed David from that day forward."* Saul knew that he had been rejected as king over Israel (see 1 Sam. 15:26), but he would not let go easily.

Later, Saul offered his daughter, Michal, to David with the dowry being killing 100

Philistines – but Saul hoped David would die trying (18:25). However, David accomplished this task, so *"Saul gave him Michal his daughter as wife. Thus Saul saw and knew that the LORD was with David…and Saul was still more afraid of David. So Saul became David's enemy continually."* (18:28-29)

The hostility continued to grow. Saul confided with his son, Jonathan, that he wanted David killed; Jonathan, being loyal to David, dissuaded his father (19:1, 4-5). The distressing spirit troubled Saul again, so David was called to soothe him with the harp… but Saul threw a spear in hopes of killing him. David escaped (19:9-10).

David was constantly on the run from Saul (19:18; 20:24, 41-42; 21:10; 23:14), until Saul finally caught up with David in En Gedi. David was able to get close enough to *"secretly cut off a corner of Saul's robe. Now it happened afterward that David's heart troubled him because he had cut Saul's robe. And he said to his men, 'The LORD forbid that I should do this thing to my master, the LORD's anointed, to stretch out my hand against him, seeing he is the anointed of the LORD"* (24:4b-6). After Saul left, David called after him and explained that David had spared Saul, even though it would have been easy to kill him. Saul's response? *"You are more righteous than I; for you have rewarded me with good, whereas I have rewarded you with evil…"* (24:17).

In 1 Samuel 26, David took one of his mighty men, Abishai, with him into Saul's camp (26:6). When they saw Saul on the ground asleep and his spear nearby, Abishai pleaded with David to allow him to kill Saul (26:7-8). It would have been so easy for David to allow this. Yet Abishai was under his command, so David responded:

"As the LORD lives, the LORD shall strike him, or his day shall come to die, or he shall go out to battle and perish. The LORD forbid that I should stretch out my hand against the LORD's anointed." (26:10-11)

So they took the spear and the jug of water by Saul's head, and they left (26:12). Here, a second time, David showed mercy to the one who was trying to kill *him.*

Second Samuel 1 records the report of Saul's death to David. David rightfully mourned for the death of Israel's leader. In the next chapter, we see David ascending the throne over Judah. (Abner, the leader of Saul's army, made Saul's son Ishbosheth king over Israel (2 Sam. 2:8-9).)

But wait. When a new king was enthroned, the custom of the time was to rid the kingdom of any enemies, anyone who may attempt to overthrow the new king or reclaim the throne. By chapter 5, Ishbosheth was killed and David was king over <u>all</u> Israel. Yet David asked this question, *"Is there still anyone who is left of the house of Saul, that I may show him kindness for Jonathan's sake?"* (2 Sam. 9:1)

Through interviewing a former servant from Saul's house, David located the son of Jonathan, Mephibosheth, and had him brought into the king's presence. The one detail we know about Mephibosheth at this point is that he was *"lame in his feet"* (9:3). David offered Mephibosheth something radical:

"Do not fear, for I will surely show you kindness for Jonathan your father's sake, and will restore to you

all the land of Saul your grandfather; and you shall eat bread at my table continually." (9:7)

Rather than doing the easy or expected thing, David was merciful to Mephibosheth. *"So Mephibosheth dwelt in Jerusalem, for he ate continually at the king's table. And he was lame in both his feet."* (9:13)

Blessing of David

_________, the LORD invites us to seek Him. If we seek Him with all our heart, He will be found (Jer. 29:13). He wants our obedience. He wants us to follow Him. He is merciful to us, sinners who deserve nothing but death (Rom. 3:23, 6:23).

I pray for you, _________, that you would extend mercy to your "enemies," just as David did. After he was anointed king, David did not overthrow King Saul in order to take his rightful place as king. No, he waited. He continued doing what he had been doing, knowing that the LORD was with him, and He would determine the downfall of Saul. Saul sought to kill David, yet when the opportunity arose for David to kill Saul, he chose not to. He continued to respect Saul's authority, even when it didn't make sense. Then, after Saul's death, David intentionally sought out anyone who was left from Saul's household. He welcomed Jonathan's son, Mephibosheth, to the king's table and cared for him there. He was merciful when it was "normal" to be vengeful.

May you seek opportunities to extend mercy to those who do not deserve it from you. Choose to be different, to show kindness rather than taking revenge. God is honored when we walk worthy of Christ and His calling.

Elijah – Zealous

Meaning: My God is Jehovah

1 Kings 17-18

Our names hold great significance. When his parents named Elijah, they were declaring to him and all who would encounter Elijah ONE thing: YHWH (Yahweh/Jehovah) is God. It's rather unlikely that Elijah's parents knew all of what their son would do, but it is amazing to see how his name spoke of who he would become and what he would declare.

Elijah comes onto the scene by declaring a drought in the land of Israel – a drought that would last 3 years (1 Kings 17:1). In the meantime, the LORD sent him to Zarephath to the home of a widow. Elijah had a simple request: water in a cup and a morsel of bread. The widow, sounding a bit destitute, replied that all she had was a little flour and oil – barely enough for herself and her son. To this, Elijah said:

"Do not fear; go and do as you have said, but make me a small cake from it first, and bring it to me; and afterward make some for yourself and your son. For thus says the L*ORD God of Israel: 'The bin of flour*

shall not be used up, nor shall the jar of oil run dry, until the day the LORD *sends rain on the earth.'"* (17:13-14)

It happened just as he had said:

So she went away and did according to the word of Elijah; and she and he and her household ate for many days. The bin of flour was not used up, nor did the jar of oil run dry, according to the word of the LORD *which He spoke by Elijah.* (17:15-16)

Later, Elijah confronted the prophets of Baal on Mount Carmel. He challenged them to show whose God was ultimate, knowing full well that YHWH would come through. They prepared two bulls and placed them on the altars – one for the 450 priests of Baal, one for Elijah. The prophets of Baal prepared theirs and offered it… with no response:

And so it was, at noon, that Elijah mocked them and said, "Cry aloud, for he is a god; either he is meditating, or he is busy, or he is on a journey, or perhaps he is sleeping and must be awakened." So they cried aloud, and cut themselves, as was their custom, with knives and lances, until the blood gushed out on them. And when midday was past, they prophesied until the time of the offering of the evening sacrifice. But there was no voice; no one answered, no one paid attention. (18:27-29)

Elijah built an altar, made a trench around the edge, cut up the bull, and placed it on the altar. Then he requested FOUR waterpots be filled and poured on the sacrifice... THREE times.

And it came to pass, at the time of the offering of the evening sacrifice, that Elijah the prophet came near and said, "LORD God of Abraham, Isaac, and Israel, let it be known this day that You are God in Israel and I am Your servant, and that I have done all these things at Your word. Hear me, O LORD, hear me, that this people may know that You are the LORD God, and that You have turned their hearts back to You again."

Then the fire of the LORD fell and consumed the burnt sacrifice, and the wood and the stones and the dust, and it licked up the water that was in the trench. Now when all the people saw it, they fell on their faces; and they said, "The LORD, He is God! The LORD, He is God!" (18:36-39)

Did you catch that? At the end the people were shouting the very meaning of Elijah's name. Why? Because he had provided God the opportunity, in the midst of many witnesses, to show His glory. Elijah didn't do it for personal gain. He did it in his zeal for the LORD. (He also executed all 450 prophets of Baal. Zealous may have been an understatement!)

In his discussion of prayer, James notes Elijah's zeal:

The effective, fervent prayer of a righteous man avails much. Elijah was a man with a nature like ours, and he prayed earnestly that it would not rain; and it did not rain on the land for three years and six months. And he prayed again, and the heaven gave rain, and the earth produced its fruit. (James 5:16b-18)

Blessing of Elijah

__________, you were created to glorify God. There are many ways you can glorify God – through your thoughts, your words, and your actions. The choices you make show others what is most important to you, so choose wisely.

I pray for you, __________, that your faith would be strong, unshakeable faith. That your heart would not envy sinners but that you would be zealous for the Lord (Prov. 23:17), just as Elijah was. He entered some seemingly impossible situations – the widow's low supply of oil and flour, the challenge of 450 prophets of Baal, confronting King Ahab and King Ahaziah with Truth. Yet in each of these situations, he trusted God to be all He says He is. I pray that you will trust God to be all He says He is – even when it doesn't make sense.

May the God who showed Himself mightily in the widow's oil and at the altar on Mount Carmel show Himself mightily in your life – not ultimately for your faith but for His glory. Ready yourself to witness some great things God has in store!

Micaiah – Steadfast

Meaning: Who is like God?

1 Kings 22, 2 Chronicles 18

King Jehoshaphat joined forces with King Ahab, yet Jehoshaphat requested they ask for the word of the LORD. Ahab attempted to forge on ahead, but Jehoshaphat persisted. As a messenger was sent to call on Micaiah, other prophets prophesied,

"Go up to Ramoth Gilead and prosper, for the LORD will deliver it into the king's hand." (1 Kings 22:12)

The messenger reported to Micaiah that these prophets had encouraged the king, and he requested Micaiah do likewise. Micaiah responded, *"As the LORD lives, whatever the LORD says to me, that I will speak."* (22:14)

And he did so. He explained to King Ahab what he saw:

"I saw all Israel scattered on the mountains, as sheep that have no shepherd. And the LORD said, 'These have no master. Let each return to his house in peace.'…Therefore hear the word of the LORD: I saw the LORD sitting on His throne, and all the host of

heaven standing on His right hand and His left. And the LORD said, 'Who will persuade Ahab king of Israel to go up, that he may fall at Ramoth Gilead?' So one spoke in this manner, and another spoke in that manner. Then a spirit came forward and stood before the LORD, and said, 'I will persuade him.' The LORD said to him, 'In what way?' So he said, 'I will go out and be a lying spirit in the mouth of all his prophets.' And the LORD said, 'You shall persuade him and also prevail; go out and do so.'

Therefore look! The LORD has put a lying spirit in the mouth of these prophets of yours, and the LORD has declared disaster against you." (22:17, 19-23)

Ahab had Micaiah imprisoned "*until I return in peace.*"(22:27)

But Micaiah refuted that small phrase: "*If you ever return in peace, the LORD has not spoken by me.*" (1 Kings 22:28a, 2 Chron. 18:27)

Ahab died in battle. (22:35)

Blessing of Micaiah

__________, let your light shine before men, that they may see your good works and glorify your Father in heaven (Matt. 5:16). You have an incredible privilege to testify to the good things God has done and is doing in your life.

I pray for you, __________, that you would be steadfast and firm in your conviction to follow God, just as Micaiah was. He faced a difficult decision – agree with the other prophets and say what the king wanted to hear or disagree and speak the truth, which could mean he'd end up in prison. He chose to speak the truth, knowing that God is the ultimate judge and it is better to offend an earthly king than the Heavenly one. Micaiah spoke what was unpopular and suffered for it, but he was obedient and loyal to the LORD.

"May your speech always be with grace, seasoned with salt, that you may know how you ought to answer each one." (Col. 4:6)

Josiah – Repentant
Meaning: Whom Jehovah Heals
2 Kings 22-23

Just a boy. Eight years old. Could you imagine becoming king at that age? Josiah did. In fact, his reign had been prophesied (1 Kings 13:2); it was no mere happenstance. His royal heritage had been tainted with idol worship. In fact, his father Amon *"forsook the LORD God of his fathers, and did not walk in the way of the LORD."* (2 Kings 21:22)

But God called Josiah out from that lineage and set him apart:

"Josiah was eight years old when he became king, and he reigned thirty-one years in Jerusalem…And he did what was right in the sight of the LORD, and walked in all the ways of his father David; he did not turn aside to the right hand or to the left." (22:1-2)

During the 18th year of his reign, King Josiah was given the Book of the Law, found by the high priest at the time. Josiah had the words read to him, and Scripture recounts, *"he tore his clothes. Then the king commanded Hilkiah the priest…saying, 'Go, inquire of the LORD for me, for the people and for all Judah, concerning the words of this book that has been found; for great is the wrath of the LORD that is aroused against us because our fathers have not obeyed the words of this book, to do according to all that is written concerning us.'"* (22:11b-13)

Huldah, the prophetess, reported: *"Thus says the LORD God of Israel: 'Concerning the words which you have heard—because your heart was tender, and you humbled yourself before the LORD when you heard what I spoke against this place and against its inhabitants…I also have heard you,' says the LORD. 'Surely, therefore, I will gather you to your fathers, and you shall be gathered to your grave in peace; and your eyes shall not see all the calamity which I will bring on this place.'"* (22:18b-20)

Josiah didn't stop what he was doing and take comfort in God's words. He didn't become lazy, knowing that God had promised he would be spared. Instead, he gathered the elders, they went to the house of the LORD, and he *"read in their hearing all the words of the Book of the Covenant which had been found in the house of the LORD."* (23:2)

The king entered covenant with the LORD, "*to follow the LORD and to keep His commandments and His testimonies and His statues, with all his heart and all his soul, to perform the words of this covenant that were written in this book.*" (23:3)

He commanded that all "*the articles that were made for Baal, for Asherah, and for all the host of heaven*" be removed from the temple. He didn't just have them removed though; "*he burned them outside Jerusalem*" (23:4). He removed the idol priests that previous kings had instated; he removed the wooden idol from the house of the LORD, burned it, and ground it to ashes (23:5-6). The "ritual booths" for this idol were torn down; the high places that had been places to worship and offer incense to the idols were demolished as well. (23:7-8)

He totally upended all the efforts the kings before him had made in dedicating places, animals, and things to the sun and other gods (23:10-14). He would leave no remnants of Israel's unfaithfulness standing. Nothing.

He restored the Passover feast to his people; "*such a Passover surely had never been held since the days of the judges who judged Israel, nor in all the days of the kings of Israel and the kings of Judah."* (23:22)

Josiah had quite the legacy. God honored him: *"Now before him there was no king like him, who turned to the LORD with all his heart, with all his soul, and with all his might, according to all the Law of Moses; nor after him did any arise like him."* (23:25)

Blessing of Josiah

_________, God has called you out in this generation to honor and glorify Him. He has called you to turn from the idol worship of those around us – whether money, self, or something else. He has called you to return to true worship.

I pray for you, _________, that your ears and heart would be open to hear the Word of the LORD, just as King Josiah's were. The Book of the Covenant had been lost, but when it was found, Josiah didn't shrug it off. He didn't only read bits and pieces. He heard the entire thing, and then responded. He repented of Judah's failure to keep covenant by tearing down anything that did not encourage worship of the One True God. I pray God's Word would have the same effect in your life.

May the God of grace show you the ways that you have strayed. May He call you lovingly back to His side, so that you can't help but leave behind those distractions and idols. To Him be the glory, great things He has done!

Solomon – Wisdom

Meaning: Peace

1 Chronicles 22, 2 Chronicles 1

As I read 1 and 2 Chronicles, the LORD revealed an awesome blessing "connection" in the life of Solomon. In 1 Chronicles 22:7-13, we see David charge Solomon with the task of building the temple David had designed for God. In the midst of this charge, there is an **extremely** important blessing:

And David said to Solomon: "My son, as for me, it was in my mind to build a house to the name of the Lord my God; but the word of the Lord came to me, saying, 'You have shed much blood and have made great wars; you shall not build a house for My name, because you have shed much blood on the earth in My sight.

Behold, a son shall be born to you, who shall be a man of rest; and I will give him rest from all his enemies all around. His name shall be Solomon, for I will give peace and quietness to Israel in his days.

He shall build a house for My name, and he shall be My son, and I will be his Father; and I will establish the throne of his kingdom over Israel forever.' Now, my son, may the Lord be with you; and may you prosper, and build the house of the Lord your God, as He has said to you. ***Only may the Lord give you wisdom and understanding, and give you charge concerning Israel, that you may keep the law of the Lord your God. Then you will prosper, if you take care to fulfill the statutes and judgments with which the Lord charged Moses concerning Israel.*** *Be strong and of good courage; do not fear nor be dismayed..."* (emphasis added)

In 2 Chronicles 1, we find a more complete understanding of the impact David's blessing had on Solomon's life:

On that night God appeared to Solomon, and said to him, "Ask! What shall I give you?"

And Solomon said to God: "You have shown great mercy to David my father, and have made me king in his place.Now, O Lord God, let Your promise to David my father be established, for You have made me king over a people like the dust of the earth in multitude. Now ***give me wisdom and knowledge****, that I may go out and come in before this people; for who can judge this great people of Yours?"*

Then God said to Solomon: "Because this was in your heart, and you have not asked riches or wealth or honor or the life of your enemies, nor have you asked long life—but have asked wisdom and knowledge for yourself, that you may judge My people over whom I have made you king—wisdom and knowledge are granted to you; and I will give you riches and wealth and honor, such as none of the kings have had who were before you, nor shall any after you have the like." (1:7-12, emphasis added)

Have you ever thought it a little odd that Solomon requested wisdom? It does seem a bit out-of-the-blue. Of course, it's an admirable quality, but... very few would request it almost instinctively. But look at this connection: David **spoke** wisdom and understanding over Solomon, so THAT is what Solomon's heart desired. When given the opportunity to choose anything, he desired to have **wisdom and understanding in ruling God's people.** He had been empowered to prosper in God's ways by his father, who probably didn't fully grasp the significance those words would have in Solomon's life.

The blessing isn't just for people who lived in the era of the Bible; it's an eternal way God operates. Let's return to the tradition of intentional blessing and see God do great things in our lives and the lives of our loved ones, just as we've seen Him do in Solomon's life.

Blessing of Solomon

__________, God has great plans for your life. He wants you to seek Him above all else, and He wants to grant you the desire of your heart (Ps. 37:4).

I pray that you, __________, would seek the LORD with all your heart. In seeking Him, you will be seeking the Ultimate Source of wisdom and understanding. May God grant to you this wisdom and discernment as He did with Solomon - not of this world but directly from His Word. May He give you the willingness to apply the wisdom you gain to your everyday life in order to be a testimony to others of the grace of God.

For the Lord gives wisdom; from His mouth come knowledge and understanding; He stores up sound wisdom for the upright; He is a shield to those who walk uprightly. (Prov. 2:6-7) *The fear of the Lord is the beginning of wisdom, and the knowledge of the Holy One is understanding.* (Prov. 9:10)

Asa – Peace

Meaning: Healer

2 Chronicles 14-15

The kings of Israel and Judah... Some were good, some were not-so-good. It's easy to overlook the kings because, let's face it, it can get downright confusing as to who is who! But Asa... Asa stands out.

Asa's father Abijam (*Abijah* in 2 Chronicles 14) "*walked in all the sins of his father...his heart was not loyal to the LORD his God*" (1 Kings 15:3). Great legacy to inherit, huh? His name, though, means **physician**. One who would bring healing. Throughout his reign, Asa is noted for his loyalty to God:

Asa did what was good and right in the eyes of the Lord his God, for he removed the altars of the foreign gods and the high places, and broke down the sacred pillars and cut down the wooden images. He commanded Judah to seek the Lord God of their fathers, and to observe the law and the commandment. He also removed the high places and the incense altars from all the cities of Judah, and the kingdom was quiet under him. And he built fortified cities in Judah, for the land had rest; he had no war in those years, because the Lord had given him rest. (2 Chron. 14:2-6)

Then, after 10 years of rest, the Ethiopians attacked with an army almost double the size of Judah's. Rather than becoming afraid and retreating, Asa cried out to the LORD:

"Lord, it is nothing for You to help, whether with many or with those who have no power; help us, O Lord our God, for we rest on You, and in Your name we go against this multitude. O Lord, You are our God; do not let man prevail against You!" (2 Chron. 14:11)

The LORD answered his cry and struck the Ethiopians. They fled, and Judah's army pursued them, eventually overthrowing them and taking "*very much spoil*" (14:13) including "*sheep and camels in abundance.*" (14:15)

After this, the prophet Azariah, under the Spirit's direction, spoke with King Asa, encouraging him to seek the LORD and not forsake Him (2 Chron. 15:1-7). Asa resolved to act:

...he took courage, and removed the abominable idols from all the land of Judah and Benjamin and from the cities which he had taken in the mountains of

Ephraim; and he restored the altar of the Lord that was before the vestibule of the Lord...

So they gathered together at Jerusalem in the third month, in the fifteenth year of the reign of Asa. And they offered to the Lord at that time seven hundred bulls and seven thousand sheep from the spoil they had brought. Then they entered into a covenant to seek the Lord God of their fathers with all their heart and with all their soul; and whoever would not seek the Lord God of Israel was to be put to death, whether small or great, whether man or woman. Then they took an oath before the Lord with a loud voice, with shouting and trumpets and rams' horns. And all Judah rejoiced at the oath, for they had sworn with all their heart and sought Him with all their soul; and He was found by them, and the Lord gave them rest all around. (15:8, 10-15)

That rest lasted 15 years, until Asa entered a treaty with the king of Syria to deal with the king of Israel. Hanani the seer rebuked Asa for doing this rather than relying on the LORD (16:7-9). Even though he faltered near the end of his reign and life, 1 Kings records him this way:

Asa did what was right in the eyes of the Lord, as did his father David. And he banished the perverted persons from the land, and removed all the idols that his fathers had made. Also he removed Maachah his grandmother from being queen mother, because she had made an obscene image of Asherah. And Asa cut down her obscene image and burned it by the Brook Kidron. But the high places were not removed. Nevertheless Asa's heart was loyal to the Lord all his days... (15:11-14)

Blessing of Asa

__________, God sees you as significant in His plan, even if the world doesn't notice your existence. Your life is another opportunity for Him to display His majesty and receive even more glory. What a privilege to honor God in that way!

I pray that you, __________, would seek God as your peace, like King Asa did in the beginning of his reign. Asa's heart was loyal to God. When the Ethiopians were attacking and Asa could have been very afraid, he chose to cry out to God - knowing that "it is nothing for God to help." It isn't difficult for Him, and He enjoys helping those who seek Him and give Him the glory. Asa's trust in God brought the kingdom of Judah many years of rest (peace) during his reign. I pray that you would trust God fully to act mightily on your behalf.

You can choose to get caught up in fear, anxiety, and stress or you can trust God for His peace. His way is better; seek Him. "The Lord will fight for you, and you shall hold your peace." (Ex. 14:14)

Nehemiah – Boldness

Meaning: Jehovah Comforts

Nehemiah 1-2

Nehemiah was the cupbearer for King Artaxerxes. News came to him that Jerusalem's walls and gates were in shambles. He was so saddened by this that he fasted, wept, and pleaded with God to keep His promise of restoration.

And I said: "I pray, Lord God of heaven, O great and awesome God, You who keep Your covenant and mercy with those who love You and observe Your commandments, please let Your ear be attentive and Your eyes open, that You may hear the prayer of Your servant which I pray before You now, day and night, for the children of Israel Your servants, and confess the sins of the children of Israel which we have sinned against You. Both my father's house and I have sinned. We have acted very corruptly against You, and have not kept the commandments, the statutes, nor the ordinances which You commanded Your servant Moses. Remember, I pray, the word that You commanded Your servant Moses, saying, 'If you are unfaithful, I will scatter you among the nations; but if you return to Me, and keep My commandments and do them, though some of you were cast out to the farthest part of the heavens, yet I will gather them from there, and bring them to the place which I have chosen as a dwelling for My name.' Now these are Your servants and Your people, whom You have redeemed by Your great power, and by Your strong hand. O Lord, I pray, please let Your ear be attentive to the prayer of Your servant, and to the prayer of Your servants who desire to fear Your name; and let Your servant prosper this day, I pray, and grant him mercy in the sight of this man." (Neh. 1:5-11a)

Later, we find Nehemiah in the king's presence, performing the duties of cupbearer. His demeanor had changed; the king noticed and questioned him. We see that Nehemiah prayed quickly and then responded with what was troubling him... and what he would like to do about it.

So I became dreadfully afraid, and said to the king, "May the king live forever! Why should my face not be sad, when the city, the place of my fathers' tombs, lies waste, and its gates are burned with fire?"

Then the king said to me, "What do you request?"

So I prayed to the God of heaven. And I said to the king, "If it pleases the king, and if your servant has found favor in your sight, I ask that you send me to Judah, to the city of my fathers' tombs, that I may rebuild it."

Then the king said to me (the queen also sitting beside him), "How long will your journey be? And when will you return?" So it pleased the king to send me; and I set him a time.

Furthermore I said to the king, "If it pleases the king, let letters be given to me for the governors of the region beyond the River, that they must permit me to pass through till I come to Judah, and a letter to Asaph the keeper of the king's forest, that he must give me timber to make beams for the gates of the citadel which pertains to the temple, for the city wall, and for the house that I will occupy." And the king granted them to me according to the good hand of my God upon me. (Neh. 2:2b-8)

Both of these instances took incredible faith, which Nehemiah obviously had. He approached both thrones boldly - knowing what God had promised and asking the king to be involved in His fulfillment of that promise.

Nehemiah encountered many obstacles while in Jerusalem, but he remained steadfast, his focus unhindered.

Blessing of Nehemiah

__________, I am so thankful for your life. God has placed you at this time in history for His glory. He has great plans for your life.

I pray that you, __________, would have boldness like Nehemiah. That you would diligently search out the Scriptures for God's promises and then boldly ask God to fulfill those promises. That you would be so aware of God's promises that when unbelievers have the opportunity to partner with you to accomplish His Word, you would have the boldness to ask them.

I also pray for wisdom with your boldness. Boldness alone can be dangerous, but when accompanied by wisdom, the LORD can bring great outcomes for His glory. Draw ever nearer to the Source of all Wisdom, God Himself.

Mordecai – Integrity

Meaning: Little Man

Esther 2-8

We are introduced to Mordecai in a paragraph that says his great grandfather (Kish) had been taken captive by King Nebuchadnezzar. The same paragraph also says,

And Mordecai had brought up Hadassah, that is, Esther, his uncle's daughter, for she had neither father nor mother. The young woman was lovely and beautiful. When her father and mother died, Mordecai took her as his own daughter. (Esther 2:7)

Mordecai's adoption of his cousin is one of the few adoptions mentioned in Scripture. In the story of Esther, King Ahasuerus had disposed of his wife, Queen Vashti, and sought a new queen. Esther had been taken to the palace, along with many other young women, to be included in those from whom the king would select his new queen. Mordecai's love and care for Esther is obvious:

And every day Mordecai paced in front of the court of the women's quarters, to learn of Esther's welfare and what was happening to her. (2:11)

Esther was chosen as the new queen. In the meantime, Mordecai discovered a plot by two doorkeepers to assassinate the king. He passed on this information to Queen Esther, who told the king. The king then had the two men hanged.

The king's second-in-command, Haman, hated the Jews – so much so that he sought to annihilate them. Mordecai found out about this also and tore his clothes and put on sackcloth and ashes (the customary sign of mourning). Through a messenger, Mordecai relayed the information to Esther about what Haman planned to do and asked her to approach the king, pleading for her people. Esther was hesitant, because entering the king's presence without his summons could mean death. Mordecai urged Esther all the more:

"Do not think in your heart that you will escape in the king's palace any more than all the other Jews. For if you remain completely silent at this time, relief and deliverance will arise for the Jews from another place, but you and your father's house will perish. Yet who knows whether you have come to the kingdom for such a time as this?" (4:13-14)

Mordecai refused to "stand or tremble" in the presence of Haman, which angered Haman. He sought to have Mordecai hanged.

The king couldn't sleep one night and had the records of the chronicles (of the kingdom) read aloud. The story of the two doorkeepers Mordecai had turned in came up, and the king asked what was done for Mordecai's loyalty. Nothing. Nothing had been done. So the next day, the king asked Haman for an idea – *"What shall be done for the man whom the king delights to honor?"* (6:6) In Haman's self-centeredness, he suggested "the man" wear the royal crest and robe, ride horseback in the city square, and have one of the princes declare that this is how the king honors men, all the while assuming the king would do such for him. What a surprise when the king did this for Mordecai, and Haman was the one declaring to the crowds!

Haman ended up being hanged on the gallows he had built to hang Mordecai (7:10). After that, the king gave Mordecai his signet ring, and Esther appointed Mordecai over the house of Haman (8:2). His willingness to go unnoticed for a time, to speak the hard truths, and to encourage Esther to do what was necessary to save her people ultimately gained him a place of high authority within the kingdom.

Blessing of Mordecai

__________, the LORD has great plans for you. He delights in you and desires for you to succeed spiritually, relationally, financially, physically, and emotionally.

I pray for you, __________, that you would be a man/woman of integrity, as Mordecai was. In his wisdom, Mordecai informed Esther of the doorkeepers' plot to kill the king. In his patience, he encouraged Esther to make the hard choice for the sake of her people, the Jews. In his humility, he did not demand repayment for saving the king but waited for his reward. Indeed, he was given a much greater reward than he had probably imagined – he became second-in-command over the kingdom after Haman was hanged. I pray you will display such wisdom, patience, and humility as you speak the truth in love – even when it hurts.

May you be led by the Holy Spirit into all truth (John 16:13) and may you eagerly follow. May your path be one of integrity for God's ultimate glory.

Daniel – Faithfulness

Meaning: God is My Judge

Daniel 1-6

Babylon has taken Judah's inhabitants captive. At the instruction of the king, Nebuchadnezzar, the finest young men - from Judah, the king's descendants, and the nobles – were to be educated in the way of the Chaldeans, in order for them to be fit to serve in the king's palace.

The young men were given wine and delicacies from the king's table during their three years of training. But then there was Daniel and his three friends (Hananiah, Mishael, and Azariah).

But Daniel purposed in his heart that he would not defile himself with the portion of the king's delicacies, nor with the wine which he drank; therefore he requested of the chief of the eunuchs that he might not defile himself. (Daniel 1:8)

Daniel proposed to the chief of the eunuchs (who was in charge of Daniel's training) that he and his three friends be tested for 10 days, eating only vegetables and drinking only water.

Though skeptical, the chief agreed. At the end of 10 days, he found the group be much healthier than those enjoying wine and delicacies.

As for these four young men, God gave them knowledge and skill in all literature and wisdom; and Daniel had understanding in all visions and dreams.

Now at the end of the days, when the king had said that they should be brought in, the chief of the eunuchs brought them in before Nebuchadnezzar. Then the king interviewed them, and among them all none was found like Daniel, Hananiah, Mishael, and Azariah; therefore they served before the king. (Daniel 1:17-19)

Daniel was given the opportunity to interpret two dreams of Nebuchadnezzar's - dreams that no other court magician or soothsayer could decipher - through God's revelation. As a result, the king praises Daniel's God as "*the revealer of secrets*" (2:47) and that "*His kingdom is from generation to generation.*" (4:34)

Later, during the reign of Darius, Daniel was the target of some of the other authorities.

So the governors and satraps sought to find some charge against Daniel concerning the kingdom; but they could find no charge or fault, because he was faithful; nor was there any error or fault found in him. Then these men said, "We shall not find any charge against this Daniel unless we find it against him concerning the law of his God." (6:4-5)

So the authorities petitioned the king to establish a 30 day edict where anyone who sought a god or man other than the king would be thrown into the lions' den (6:6-9). By declaring this, the authorities knew that they would be able to trap Daniel because **he was faithful.**

Sure enough, Daniel endured (6:11). The authorities presented their case before King Darius, who had no choice but to uphold his word and throw Daniel into the lions' den (6:14-15). However, because of his **faithfulness**:

Then Daniel said to the king, "O king, live forever! My God sent His angel and shut the lions' mouths, so that they have not hurt me, because I was found innocent before Him; and also, O king, I have done no wrong before you." (6:21-22)

Yet again, a pagan king praises God through Daniel's witness (6:26-27). What a legacy.

Blessing of Daniel

_________, you are an image-bearer of God, created to bring Him glory. He deserves all the glory because He is God. What a privilege it is to be a vessel for the LORD and for Him to choose you to bring Him glory.

I pray that you, _________, would be faithful to God through trying times, just as Daniel was. He was taken captive at a young age, yet even in a foreign land, he remained faithful to God. He purposed in his heart that he would not defile himself. His faithfulness was so evident that pagan kings praised his God! His faithfulness was so evident that other authorities had to attack his relationship with God, because there was no other fault in him. He clung to the LORD in an uncertain land; I pray that you will cling to God even now.

Purpose in your heart, even now, to not defile yourself. May your relationship with God be so close and your testimony of His goodness so grand that there is no question Who you serve. May you be a strong, faithful vessel for His glory.

New Testament

Peter - Unashamed
Philip – Words of Life
Stephen - Sacrifice
Paul - Humility
Cornelius - Willing
Barnabas - Encouragement

Peter – Unashamed

Meaning: A Rock or a Stone

Acts 3-4, 9

Bold seems to be an understatement for Peter. From his mouth came forth the declarations, *"Even if all are made to stumble because of You [Jesus], I will never be made to stumble"* and *"Even if I have to die with You, I will not deny You!"* (Matt. 26:33, 35) Just a few short verses later in Matthew, we see Peter deny Jesus three times and weep bitterly. His pride backfired.

Three days later, a group of women visited the tomb of Jesus, to prepare His body for burial. They found an empty tomb and ran to tell the disciples (Luke 24:1-11). Peter ran to the tomb to see for himself, and *"stopping down, he saw the linen cloths lying by themselves; and he departed, marveling to himself at what at happened"* (Luke 24:12). Lo and behold, Jesus had risen – just as He'd promised.

After His ascension and the release of the Holy Spirit at Pentecost, Peter's boldness became an asset to the early church. He healed in the name of Christ (Acts 3:1-10)… And one such healing had a huge impact:

Now it came to pass, as Peter went through all parts of the country, that he also came down to the saints who dwelt in Lydda. There he found a certain man names Aeneas, who had been bedridden eight years and was paralyzed. And Peter said to him, "Aeneas, Jesus the Christ heals you. Arise and make your bed." Then he arose immediately. ***So all who dwelt at Lydda and Sharon saw him and turned to the Lord.*** (Acts 9:32-35, emphasis added)

It might have been easier to move right along, but Peter used the gifts the Holy Spirit had given him, and two towns were changed because of it.

After the healing in Acts 3, the crowds were *"greatly amazed."* Peter capitalized on this opportunity and preached a lengthy discourse about Christ. Here is an excerpt:

Men of Israel, why do you marvel at this? Or why look so intently at us, as though by our own power or godliness we had made this man walk? The God of Abraham, Isaac, and Jacob, the God of our fathers, glorified His Servant Jesus, whom you delivered up and denied in the presence of Pilate, when he was determined to let Him go…But those things which God foretold by the mouth of all His prophets, that the Christ would suffer, He has thus fulfilled. Repent therefore and be converted, that your sins may be blotted out, so that times of refreshing may come from the presence of the Lord, and that He may send Jesus Christ, who was preached to you before… You are sons of the prophets, and of the covenant which God made with our fathers, saying to Abraham, 'And in your seed all the families of the earth shall be blessed.' To you first, God, having raised up His Servant Jesus, sent Him to bless you, in turning away every one of you from your iniquities. (Acts 3:12-13, 18-20, 25-26)

Peter and John were arrested immediately following Peter's monologue (4:1-3). *"However, many of those who heard the word believed; and the number of the men came to be about five thousand"* (4:4). The Sanhedrin questioned Peter and John the next day, asking, *"By what power or by what name have you done this?"* (4:5-7)

Peter, filled with the Holy Spirit, responded: *"Rulers of the people and elders of Israel: If we this day are judged for a good deed done to a helpless man, by what means he has been made well, let it be known to you all, and to all the people of Israel, that by the name of Jesus Christ of Nazareth, whom you crucified, whom God raised from the dead, by Him this man stands here before you whole… Nor is there salvation in any other, for there is no other name under heaven given among men by which we must be saved."* (4:8-10, 12)

In this case, the very boldness Peter, an *"uneducated and untrained"* man, espoused created a sense of wonder in the Sanhedrin. *"And they realized that they had been with Jesus"* (4:13). Of course, this was not the end of Peter's boldness. He unashamedly proclaimed the news of salvation, and many were added to the early church as a result of his boldness.

This man who denied Jesus not once but **three** times could have been crippled by his offense. He could have become useless. Yet he did not let it define him. In fact, he well lived out the blessing Christ spoke over him: *"Blessed are you Simon Bar-Jonah, for flesh and blood has not revealed this to you, by My Father who is in heaven.*

And I also say to you that you are Peter, and on this rock I will build My church, and the gates of Hades shall not prevail against it." (Matt. 16:17-18)

Blessing of Peter

_________, your worth is not determined by your actions. Your worth has already been assigned to you, and nothing you choose to do can destroy that.

I pray for you, _________, that you would be unashamed of the Gospel and that you would readily identify yourself with Jesus Christ, just as Peter did. Yes – Peter faltered. He denied Christ three times. The wonder of it all is that God still had a plan for Peter's life. He still had a purpose that Peter would fulfill in the days of the early church. He was not deterred by Peter's actions, because Peter's worth was not determined by those actions. He was already worth the death of the Son of God. When he embraced this, Peter was a bold and strong witness for the Lord.

"Therefore gird up the loins of your mind, be sober, and rest your hope fully upon the grace that is to be brought to you at the revelation of Jesus Christ; as obedient children, not conforming yourselves to the former lusts, as in your ignorance; but as He who called you is holy, you also be holy in all your conduct, because it is written, 'Be holy, for I am holy'" (1 Pet. 1:13-16). Be bold and unashamed!

Philip – Words of Life

Meaning: Lover of Horses

Acts 8

Not to be confused with Philip the disciple of Jesus (Matthew 10:3, Mark 3:18, Luke 6:14), the Philip we meet in Acts 6 is selected to serve as a deacon of the church in Jerusalem. This role was that of caring for the widows who were being overlooked.

A couple chapters later, we find Philip in the city of Samaria, preaching Christ (8:5). The LORD used him in a mighty way in Samaria:

And the multitudes with one accord heeded the things spoken by Philip, hearing and seeing the miracles which he did. For unclean spirits, crying with a loud voice, came out of many who were possessed; and many who were paralyzed and lame were healed. And there was great joy in that city." (8:6-8)

He was eager to obey, no matter where that meant he would have to go. When an angel of the Lord spoke to him, telling him to go south on the road from Jerusalem to Gaza – which is desert – he *"arose and went"* (8:26-27). God had an appointment for Philip that day:

And behold, a man of Ethiopia, a eunuch of great authority under Candace the queen of the Ethiopians, who had charge of all her treasury, and had come to Jerusalem to worship, was returning. And sitting in his chariot, he was reading Isaiah the prophet. Then the Spirit said to Philip, "Go near and overtake this chariot." (8:27-29)

Scripture doesn't note that Philip hesitated at all. In fact, it says:

So Philip ran to him, and heard him reading the prophet Isaiah, and said, "Do you understand what you are reading?"

And he said, "How can I, unless someone guides me?" And he asked Philip to come up and sit with him. The place in the Scripture which he read was this:

> *"He was led as a sheep to the slaughter; and as a lamb before its shearer is silent, so He opened not His mouth. In His humiliation His justice was taken away, and who will declare His generation? For His life is taken from the earth."*

So the eunuch answered Philip and said, "I ask you, of whom does the prophet say this, of himself or of some other man?" (8:30-34)

Philip took this unique opportunity to preach about Christ. How? He started with this very Scripture (8:35)! They traveled together, and when they came to some water, the eunuch said, *"'See, here is water. What hinders me from being baptized?'*

Then Philip said, 'If you believe with all your heart, you may.'

And he answered and said, 'I believe that Jesus Christ is the Son of God.'

So he commanded the chariot to stand still. And both Philip and the eunuch went down into the water, and he baptized him. Now when they came up out of the water, the Spirit of the Lord caught Philip away, so that the eunuch saw him no more; and he went on his way rejoicing." (8:36-39)

Philip did not delay in obedience. He went. When the Spirit prompted him to speak to the eunuch, he *ran.* When the man asked him a question, Philip gave a timely and true answer. The Word of Life spread to a region (Ethiopia) none of the disciples traveled to. All because one man was willing to speak words of Life to a man who was dead in his sin.

Blessing of Philip

_________, "I call heaven and earth as witnesses today against you, that I have set before you life and death, blessing and cursing; therefore choose life, that both you and your descendants may live." (Deut. 30:19)

I pray for you, _________, that you would seek to speak words of Life to those around you, just as Philip did. He obeyed the call when God sent him to walk a desert road but didn't give him a final destination. Then when the Spirit prompted him to speak to a man from another country who may have spoken a different language, he did not hesitate; he ran. He found an opportunity to speak to the Ethiopian eunuch about Christ, the One who is Life.

May your words direct others to the life they can find in Christ, though they are dead in sin (Eph. 2:1). May your life be a shining example of the vibrant life God gives us as we follow Him in repentance, belief, and obedience. "Love the LORD your God…obey His voice…cling to Him, for He is your life and the length of your days." (Deut. 30:20a)

Stephen – Sacrifice
Meaning: Crowned
Acts 6-7

The apostles devoted themselves to prayer and fasting, so when the Hellenists were upset that their widows were being overlooked, the apostles charged the multitude with the task of appointing seven men to care for the widows (the very beginning of what we know as "deacons" today). Included in the chosen was Stephen, *"a man full of faith and the Holy Spirit."* (Acts 6:5)

Luke, the writer of Acts, talks about how the Spirit used Stephen:

And Stephen, full of faith and power, did great wonders and signs among the people. Then there arose some from what is called the Synagogue of the Freedmen (Cyrenians, Alexandrians, and those from Cilicia and Asia), disputing with Stephen. And they were not able to resist the wisdom and the Spirit by which he spoke. (6:8-10)

Because Stephen was merely a vessel in the hands of the omnipotent God, He accomplished great things through him. Stephen also became the focal point for contention – so much so that when he was tried before the council, the opposition set up false witnesses against him.

Stephen didn't back down from the awesome opportunity set before him. He answered his critics with a brief yet thorough explanation of their shared history and how Christ fulfilled that history. They did not accept his explanation though: *"When they heard these things they were cut to the heart, and they gnashed at him with their teeth."* (7:54)

He didn't skip a beat, though. His life was not worth more to him than Christ.

> *But he, being full of the Holy Spirit, gazed into heaven and saw the glory of God, and Jesus standing at the right hand of God, and said, "Look! I see the heavens opened and the Son of Man standing at the right hand of God!" Then they cried out with a loud voice, stopped their ears, and ran at him with one accord; and they cast him out of the city and stoned him.* (7:55-58)

Luke gives us a few more details of Stephen's death:

And they stoned Stephen as he was calling on God and saying, "Lord Jesus, receive my spirit." Then he knelt down and cried out with a loud voice, "Lord, do not charge them with this sin." And when he had said this, he fell asleep. (7:59-60)

Blessing of Stephen

_________, God delights in you. He rejoices when you pursue a relationship with Him, when you get to know Him more. He created you for His glory, and He longs for you to seek Him with all your heart.

I pray for you, _________, that you would be a vessel ready to be used by God, just as Stephen was. Stephen is known as the first martyr of the early Church – the first to die for the cause of Christ. He is noted for being full of faith and the Holy Spirit. By making Christ's agenda his, he gave many the opportunity to hear truth. Even in his death, he displayed the grace of God.

I pray your life will never be worth more to you than what God has in store. He writes life stories full of purpose and meaning, learning and growing. He never wastes any life fully surrendered to His service. May your surrender be willing and your walk be joyous.

Paul – Humility
Meaning: Small
Acts 9

At the stoning of Stephen, Luke introduces us to a peculiar young man by the name of Saul (Acts 7:58). We find out that "*Saul was consenting to his death*" and also that "*as for Saul, he made havoc of the church, entering every house, and dragging off men and women, committing them to prison*" (8:1, 3). To say he was zealous would merely scratch the surface (in fact, he admits to being zealous in Phil. 3:6).

This Saul was so zealous that he went to the high priest and asked him for letters to Damascus synagogues. Why? "*So that if he found any who were of the Way…he might bring them bound to Jerusalem*" (9:1-2). He contrived this plan for the sole purpose of discovering more Christ followers in order to imprison them.

In His sovereignty, the LORD had different plans.

"*As he journeyed he came near Damascus, and suddenly a light shone around him from heaven. Then he fell to the ground, and heard a voice saying to him, 'Saul, Saul, why are you persecuting Me?'*

And he said, 'Who are You, Lord?'

Then the Lord said, 'I am Jesus, whom you are persecuting. It is hard for you to kick against the goads.'

So he, trembling and astonished, said, 'Lord, what do you want me to do?'

Then the Lord said to him, 'Arise and go into the city, and you will be told what you must do.'" (9:3-6)

Not only does Saul have this miraculous encounter with the Risen Savior, but he was blinded. *"And he was three days without sight."* (9:9)

Saul's reputation preceded him, so when the Lord told Ananias, a believer in Damascus, Ananias was hesitant. To this hesitation, the Lord replied: *"Go, for he is a chosen vessel of Mine to bear My name before Gentiles, kings, and the children of Israel. For I will show him how many things he must suffer for My name's sake."* (9:15-16)

Ananias went, laid hands on Saul, and informed him that the Lord Jesus sent him *"that* [Saul] *may receive* [his] *sight and be filled with the*

Holy Spirit" (9:17). Scales fell from Saul's eyes, he received his sight, and he was baptized. (9:18)

In his letter to the Galatians, Saul (now known as Paul) explains what happened next:

"But when it pleased God, who separated me from my mother's womb and called me through His grace, to reveal His Son in me, that I might preach Him among the Gentiles, I did not immediately confer with flesh and blood, nor did I go up to Jerusalem to those who were apostles before me; but I went to Arabia, and returned again to Damascus. Then after three years I went up to Jerusalem to see Peter…" (Gal. 1:15-18a)

This man, an elite Jew with Pharisee education (Phil. 3:5-6), did not seek out others to teach him. He didn't go to the apostles to learn all he needed to know. No doubt, this was a huge test of his redirected faith; it went against what was so deeply ingrained in him. But he would face such friction often. After all, this elite Jew was chosen by God to bear His name *"before Gentiles*!" It was all part of the process God was using to bring Paul to a point where later he could write these words to Timothy, his son in the faith:

"And I thank Christ Jesus our Lord who has enabled me, because He counted me faithful, putting me into the ministry, although I was formerly a blasphemer, a persecutor, and an insolent man; but I obtained mercy because I did it ignorantly in unbelief. And the grace of our Lord was exceedingly abundant, with faith and love which are in Christ Jesus. This is a faithful saying and worthy of all acceptance, that Christ Jesus came into the world to save sinners, of whom I am chief. However, for this reason I obtained mercy, that in me first Jesus Christ might show all longsuffering, as a pattern to those who are going to believe on Him for everlasting life. Now to the King eternal, immortal, invisible, to God who alone is wise, be honor and glory forever and ever. Amen." (1 Timothy 1:12-17)

Blessing of Paul

__________, you have a daily choice. You can obey God and serve Him, or you can gratify your own desires and be your own god. Sometimes the second choice seems more "fun" but the first will always be more fruitful.

I pray for you, __________, that God would humble you. That your accomplishments and successes would not be where you find your value. Paul was stripped of everything he had looked to for value – his heritage, his education, his position of leadership. God did away with all the earthly qualifications he had so that Paul could focus on Who God is and what He has done in sending Jesus as the fulfillment of the longed-for Messiah. At first, Paul thought that persecuting those who followed Christ was the mission God had sent him on; how humbling it was to encounter the Risen Savior and to be converted to "His" side.

"Do nothing through selfish ambition or conceit" (Phil. 2:3-4). May the God who used a man such as Paul have full access to your heart. He is glorified when our humility is merely a means of redirecting attention to the One Who is worthy of it.

Cornelius – Willing
Meaning: Of a Horn
Acts 10

When you think of men of the Bible, Cornelius probably doesn't come to the forefront of your mind. Yet Luke, the writer of Acts, records some very intriguing details as we are introduced to this Gentile (non-Jewish) man:

There was a certain man in Caesarea called Cornelius, a centurion of what was called the Italian Regiment, a devout man and one who feared God with all his household, who gave alms generously to the people, and prayed to God always. (10:1-2)

A centurion. From Italy (likely Rome). Devout. Feared God (and led his household to do likewise). Generous. Prayerful. Wow – what descriptors! God had plans for this centurion who was stationed in Caesarea…

About the ninth hour of the day he saw clearly in a vision an angel of God coming in and saying to him, "Cornelius!"

And when he observed him, he was afraid, and said, "What is it, lord?"

So he said to him, "Your prayers and your alms have come up for a memorial before God. Now send men to Joppa, and send for Simon whose surname is Peter. He is lodging with Simon, a tanner, whose house is by the sea. He will tell you what you must do." (10:3-6)

Cornelius did just that. He sent two servants and a soldier to Joppa to retrieve Peter. While the three journeyed, the Lord was visiting Peter with a dream/vision that turned his Jewish world upside down. The foods that Peter was accustomed to viewing as "unclean" or "common" were no longer so (10:9-16). The Spirit then told Peter that the trio was on their way, and he should go with them (10:19-20). The next day, they all traveled back to Caesarea. (10:23)

In the meantime, Cornelius gathered his relatives and close friends and waited for his servants' return (10:24). *As Peter was coming in, Cornelius met him and fell down at his feet and worshiped him. But Peter lifted him up, saying, "Stand up; I myself am also a man"* (10:25-26). Peter reminded Cornelius that Jews don't associate with Gentiles, but now, God had *"shown* [him] *that* [he] *should not call any man common or unclean"* (10:28). Peter asked why Cornelius had sent for him (10:29). Cornelius recounted the visit by the angel of God, and then added "*...you have done well to come. Now therefore, we are all present before God, to hear all the things commanded you by God."* (10:33b)

Peter utilized this opportunity to speak truth to Cornelius' household and close friends. He preached *"peace through Jesus Christ"* and that *"whoever believes in Him will receive remission of sins"* (10:36, 43). Many believed and were baptized. (10:44-48)

Blessing of Cornelius

________, are you willing to hear the Word of God? Are you eager to have someone tell you about it?

I pray for you, ________, that your heart would be willing and eager to search out God's Word, just as Cornelius was willing to send for Peter. His willingness was obedience to the God of the universe. Perhaps he had an inkling of what God might do, maybe he didn't have a clue. Regardless, he responded without question, and his family tree was forever changed.

Sometimes it's the small choices to obey that have the biggest impact – not only on your generation but on the generations to come. May you obey enthusiastically, even when it seems inconvenient. God works in the little and the big acts of obedience.

Barnabas – Encouragement

Meaning: Son of Rest

Acts 11

We first encounter Barnabas in Acts 4:36-37, where Luke writes, *"And Joses, who was also named Barnabas by the apostles (which is translated Son of Encouragement), a Levite of the country of Cyprus, having land, sold it, and brought the money and laid it at the apostles' feet."* It would not be a stretch to say Barnabas was a giver. He sold land and gave the money to the early church.

Saul converted to Christianity after persecuting the church, and Barnabas escorted him to the apostles, since the disciples were afraid of Saul and disbelieved his conversion. (9:26-27)

In Acts 11, Barnabas was sent by the church at Jerusalem to Antioch to investigate preaching and conversions that were taking place as a result of Stephen's witness to the Jews (11:19-22). *"When he came and had seen the grace of God, he was glad, and encouraged them all that with purpose of heart they should continue with the Lord. For he was a good man, full of the Holy Spirit and of faith. And a great many people were added to the Lord."* (11:23-24)

Barnabas then traveled on to Tarsus, retrieved Saul, and they returned to Antioch, where they spent a year teaching the church (11:25-26). After that, they traveled to Jerusalem, where they chose John Mark to continue their journey. They returned to Antioch, where the prophets and teachers laid hands on them and then sent them on to the next stop. (13:1-3)

Later, in Antioch of Pisidia, conflict arose:

On the next Sabbath almost the whole city came together to hear the word of God. But when the Jews saw the multitudes, they were filled with envy; and contradicting and blaspheming, they opposed the things spoken by Paul. Then Paul and Barnabas grew bold and said, "It was necessary that the word of God should be spoken to you first; but since you reject it, and judge yourselves unworthy of everlasting life, behold, we turn to the Gentiles. For so the Lord has commanded us:

'I have set you as a light to the Gentiles,
That you should be for salvation to the ends of the earth.'"

Now when the Gentiles heard this, they were glad and glorified the word of the Lord. And as many as had been appointed to eternal life believed.

And the word of the Lord was being spread throughout all the region. (13:44-49)

God intended for Barnabas to encourage others; we can see that in the very meaning of his name. What an awesome task it was for him – to encourage new believers as the gospel of Christ spread.

Blessing of Barnabas

_________, God has great things in store for you. I have no doubt He desires to use your life to magnify His name, that others would see Him in you and glorify Him for it.

I pray for you, _________, that you would be known as an encourager to those around you, just as Barnabas was. He taught new believers. God's Word says he "encouraged them all that with purpose of heart they should continue with the Lord." Encouragement isn't just a pat on the back or a "Good job!" here or there. Encouragement is spurring someone on to accomplish great things for God… to learn more about Him and His ways. Sometimes, like at Antioch of Pisidia, you can encourage those who believe by speaking boldly to those who are wrong.

May you be known as an encourager. May your words be "acceptable in His sight." (Ps. 19:14) May your mouth be an instrument to encourage others for God's glory.

Women

Sarah - Faith
Deborah – Conviction
Jael – Available
Hannah – Joyful
Mary - Favor

Sarah – Faith
Meaning: Noblewoman
Genesis 17-18, 21

Barren. All her life, Sarah had been unable to bear children. There was no descendant to inherit the wealth Abraham and Sarah had received. But the God who called Abraham to a land foreign to him also promised, *"I will bless her and also give you [Abraham] a son by her; then I will bless her, and she shall be the mother of nations; kings of peoples shall be from her."* (Gen. 17:16)

Abraham laughed at the thought of it, since both of them were beyond the childbearing years (17:17). Again, God assured him Sarah would: *"…you shall call his name Isaac; I will establish My covenant with him for an everlasting covenant, and with his descendants after him."* (17:19)

In a later conversation, the LORD visited Abraham, speaking again of the promise (18:10). Sarah overheard their conversation, and *"Sarah laughed within herself"* (18:12). God asked Abraham why she laughed,

"Why did Sarah laugh, saying, 'Shall I surely bear a child, since I am old?' Is anything too hard for

the LORD? At the appointed time I will return to you, according to the time of life, and Sarah shall have a son." (18:13-14)

Genesis 21 tells us, *"And the LORD visited Sarah as He had said, and the LORD did for Sarah as He had spoken"* (21:1). They named him Isaac, just as the LORD commanded – quite applicable, too, since Isaac means "he who laughs." (21:3)

Hebrews 11 recounts Sarah's faith this way: *"By faith Sarah herself also received strength to conceive seed, and she bore a child when she was past the age, because she judged Him faithful who had promised."* (11:11)

Although Sarah's laughter at God's promise seems to be rude, inconsiderate, and lacking faith, the author of Hebrews records that she had faith. Faith that strengthened her to do the unfathomable – bear a child in her old age. Faith that found its footing in the character of the One who is faithful to fulfill all His promises.

Blessing of Sarah

__________, what a unique opportunity the LORD has given you to display His glory as a female. He has blessed you with abilities and desires in order for you to seek Him and to glorify Him in all you say and do.

I pray for you, __________, that the God who is faithful would grant you a firm faith, just as Sarah had. She did not fight God's promise, as unimaginable as it was to her. In her humanity, she saw the impossibility of having children, but Hebrews tells us she still had faith. She had faith because God is faithful. He does not make a promise He will not keep, and this strengthened Sarah. This aspect of who God is provided a solid foundation for her faith, even when her future seemed bleak.

May your faith be rooted in the LORD. May you "judge Him faithful who had promised," just as Sarah did. All of His promises are true; cling to this truth with it otherwise seems hopeless.

Deborah – Conviction

Meaning: Bee

Judges 4-5

It's the era of judges in Israel's history. Appointed by the LORD, Ehud delivered the children of Israel (who were serving the king of Moab at the time), which brought rest to the land for 80 years (Judges 3). After Ehud died, Israel returned to their evil ways -- "*So the LORD sold them into the hand of Jabin king of Canaan... The commander of his army was Sisera...*" (4:2). They weren't without a judge during their oppression though.

God raised up Deborah.

She called for Barak and said to him,

Has not the Lord God of Israel commanded, "Go and deploy troops at Mount Tabor; take with you ten thousand men of the sons of Naphtali and of the sons of Zebulun; and against you I will deploy Sisera, the commander of Jabin's army, with his chariots and his multitude at the River Kishon; and I will deliver him into your hand"? (4:6-7)

Barak responded:

If you will go with me, then I will go; but if you will not go with me, I will not go! (4:8)

He trusted in Deborah more than he trusted in God. For this, Deborah rebuked him:

I will surely go with you; nevertheless there will be no glory for you in the journey you are taking, for the Lord will sell Sisera into the hand of a woman. (4:9)

This is not a compliment. In fact, it would be an utter embarrassment for the victor to be a woman. But for God -- it would be yet another way to display His glory. Deborah told Barak to go to Mount Tabor because the LORD has delivered Sisera into his hand... so he went. Judges says, "*...all the army of Sisera fell by the edge of the sword; not a man was left*" (4:16). But not so fast...

However, Sisera had fled away on foot... (4:17)

If you read the remainder of chapter 4, you find that Jael presented Sisera with hospitality -- and then drove a tent peg through his temple. Israel grew stronger and stronger until they were able to overpower and destroy Jabin king of Canaan.

Judges 5 is the song of Deborah and Barak, rejoicing in their victory and the goodness of God. They end their song:

Thus let all Your enemies perish, O Lord!
But let those who love Him be like the sun
When it comes out in full strength. (5:31)

Blessing of Deborah

_________, God knew what He was doing when He placed you at this exact time in history. He wants you to be ready, willing, and able to make His name known among the nations – and that starts now. You have the great opportunity and privilege to be used by Him for great things.

I pray for you, _________, that you would stand firm in your convictions and call forth greatness in others, just as Deborah did. She didn't waver even though the culture of her day was in blatant rebellion against God. She did not take over the command of the army; she spurred Barak on to lead well. I pray you will hold fast to the Word of God and set your own agenda aside. God can do great things when we are willing.

May your eyes be turned from self to God and others. May your focus be on that which will bring God the most glory.

Jael – Available

Meaning: Mountain Goat

Judges 4-5

It's the era of judges in Israel's history, and Deborah is the current judge. Israel is under the oppressing rule of Jabin king of Canaan and his army commander, Sisera. God's getting ready to do something big.

Deborah called Barak, the commander of Israel's army, and charged him to send troops to Mount Tabor because the LORD has promised to deliver Sisera into Barak's hand.

Barak hesitated, requesting Deborah accompany him. For trusting in her and not fully in the LORD, Deborah rebuked Barak and informed him:

...there will be no glory for you in the journey you are taking, for the Lord will sell Sisera into the hand of a woman. (Judges 4:9)

Barak took 10,000 men with him to Mount Tabor and the LORD routed Sisera's army and chariots. "*...all the army of Sisera fell by the edge of the sword; not a man was left*" (4:16).

However, Sisera had fled away on foot to the tent of Jael, the wife of Heber the Kenite; for there was peace between Jabin king of Hazor and the house of Heber the Kenite. (4:17)

Jael was rather hospitable to Sisera. She offered him a blanket. When he requested water to drink, she brought him milk. And then he asked her to tell anyone who asked that "no man is here."

What happened next seems a bit extraordinary.

Then Jael, Heber's wife, took a tent peg and took a hammer in her hand, and went softly to him and drove the peg into his temple, and it went down into the ground; for he was fast asleep and weary. So he died. (4:21)

The unsuspecting Sisera never woke up from his nap. In chapter 5, Deborah and Barak sing a song of victory, rejoicing in the goodness of God. They recount Jael's story this way:

Most blessed among women is Jael,
The wife of Heber the Kenite;
Blessed is she among women in tents.
He asked for water, she gave milk;

She brought out cream in a lordly bowl.
She stretched her hand to the tent peg,
Her right hand to the workmen's hammer;
She pounded Sisera, she pierced his head,
She split and struck through his temple.
At her feet he sank, he fell, he lay still;
At her feet he sank, he fell;
Where he sank, there he fell dead. (5:24-27)

After this, the land had rest for 40 years. (5:31)

Blessing of Jael

_________, you are a one-of-a-kind image-bearer for the LORD. He appointed you for this time in history to impact those you interact with -- whether it is on a daily basis or a one-time encounter. He has chosen you to glorify Him in the choices you make. He is preparing you even now to do great things.

I pray for you, _________, that God would strengthen you to be a mighty vessel for Him. I pray that you would be ready to be used by God at a moment's notice, just as Jael was. Jael received great blessing by being available and being aware of what was going on. God received glory, and the land was soon at rest. He wants to use you in the same way.

Continue to seek opportunities to share in how God is working. Be ready and available for Him to work in and through you. May you walk worthy of the Lord, fully pleasing Him (Col. 1:9-12).

Hannah – Joyful
Meaning: Grace
1 Samuel 1-2

Childless. In ancient Hebrew culture, that spelled c-u-r-s-e-d. Hannah watched as her husband Elkanah's other wife, Peninnah, had children… but the LORD had closed Hannah's womb (1 Samuel 1:2, 5). Scripture explains that Peninnah *"provoked* [Hannah] *severely, to make her miserable, because the LORD had closed her womb"* (1:6). This happened on a yearly basis, to the point where Hannah *"wept and did not eat."* (1:7)

Elkanah tried to comfort her (1:8), but he could not. She desperately longed for a child: *"And she was in bitterness of soul, and prayed to the LORD and wept in anguish. Then she made a vow and said, 'O LORD of hosts, if You will indeed look on the affliction of Your maidservant and remember me, and not forget Your maidservant, but will give Your maidservant a male child, then I will give him to the LORD all the days of his life, and no razor shall come upon his head"* (1:10-11). She was consecrating her firstborn, setting him apart with the Nazirite vow – and he had not even been conceived.

Had the LORD forgotten or overlooked Hannah?

Eli the priest was nearby as Hannah cried out. Thinking she was drunk, he confronted her on this (1:14). She replied that she was not drunk, she was *"a woman of sorrowful spirit."* She had *"poured out* [her] *soul before the LORD"* and *"out of the abundance of* [her] *complaint and grief* [she had] *spoken until now."* (1:15-16)

Eli answered her: *"Go in peace, and the God of Israel grant your petition which you have asked of Him."* Having received this grand blessing, she *"went her way and ate, and her face was no longer sad."* (1:17-18)

Hannah conceived and gave birth to a son. She named him Samuel, which means, "His name is El (God)." The first ten verses of 1 Samuel 2 record Hannah's prayer of thanksgiving and rejoicing over what God had done in her life. She had experienced His provision first-hand, and she was confident in the LORD's goodness.

Blessing of Hannah

__________, the LORD chose for you to be a girl/woman. He did not make a mistake; you were not supposed to be a boy. He placed you in this time in history as a girl/woman to bring Him glory as only you can.

I pray for you, __________, that your heart would desire to see the LORD's provision in your life, just as Hannah did. Hannah longed for a son, and she poured out the desire before Him. She did not understand why she had no children, but she knew Who to turn to. And so she pleaded with Him for the fulfillment of that desire, willing to sacrifice that desire and dedicate her son to serve in the temple rather than to have no son at all. I pray you will seek the LORD for His provision.

May the God who provided Hannah with the son she so desperately wanted provide for YOU a godly legacy. In every circumstance of His provision, may you praise Him out loud to those around you.

Mary – Favor
Meaning: Their Rebellion
Luke 1

Young. That's what Mary was when the angel Gabriel visited her (Luke 1:26). Some sources think she could be as young as 13 or 14. Imagine… God sent an angel to a teenager, and the angel said, *"Rejoice, highly favored one, the Lord is with you; blessed are you among women!"* (1:28)

It's not surprising that Mary was *"troubled at his saying"* (1:29); such a message would be overwhelming, to say the least. The angel continued, *"Do not be afraid, Mary, for you have found favor with God. And behold, you will conceive in your womb and bring forth a Son, and shall call His name JESUS…"* (1:30-31)

But how?? She was a virgin.

"And the angel answered and said to her, 'The Holy Spirit will come upon you, and the power of the Highest will overshadow you; therefore, also, that Holy One who is to be born will be called the Son of God. Now indeed, Elizabeth your relative has also conceived a son in her old age; and this is now the

sixth month for her who was called barren. For with God nothing is impossible." (1:35-37)

I can almost hear the excitement in Mary's reply: *"Behold the maidservant of the Lord! Let it be to me according to your word."* (1:38)

Mary went to visit her cousin, Elizabeth. Upon Mary's arrival, Elizabeth was *"filled with the Holy Spirit"* (1:41). The words from Elizabeth's mouth poured forth blessing:

"Blessed are you among women, and blessed is the fruit of your womb! But why is this granted to me, that the mother of my Lord should come to me? For indeed, as soon as the voice of your greeting sounded in my ears, the babe leaped in my womb for joy. Blessed is she who believed, for there will be a fulfillment of those things which were told her from the Lord." (1:42-45)

Mary's response to both the favor of the Lord and the blessing from Elizabeth was that of praise. Luke records her full praise in chapter one, verses 46-55. Here is an excerpt of that:

For He has regarded the lowly state of His maidservant; for behold, henceforth all generations will call me blessed. For He who is mighty has done great things for me, and holy is His name. And His mercy is on those who fear Him from generation to generation. (1:48-50)

Blessing of Mary

_________, the LORD uses the foolish things of the world to put to shame the wise (1 Cor. 1:27). "According to the flesh, not many mighty, not many noble, are called." (1 Cor. 1:26). He operates contrary to the patterns of those around us.

I pray for you, _________, that you would realize the favor God has granted you, as He granted Mary favor. She had the one-of-a-kind privilege to carry the Son of God, the long-promised Savior and to be His mother. No, you will not have that kind of privilege, but you have been given the task of shining as a light in a dark world. You have been called out of the darkness into His marvelous light; don't keep that to yourself!

"The foolishness of God is wiser than men" (1 Cor. 1:25a). He knew what He was doing when He chose Mary to bring forth Christ into the world. He knew what He was doing when He called you "favored," one who will bring the Good News to those around you. "Humble yourself in the sight of the Lord, and He will lift you up." (James 4:10)

Scripture to Use for Blessing

Now therefore, if you will indeed obey My voice and keep My covenant, then you shall be a special treasure to Me above all people; for all the earth is Mine. And you shall be to Me a kingdom of priests and a holy nation. –Exodus 19:5-6a

Then the LORD spoke to Moses, saying, "Speak to the children of Israel, and say to them: 'I am the LORD your God. According to the doings of the land of Egypt, where you dwelt, you shall not do; and according to the doings of the land of Canaan, where I am bringing you, you shall not do; nor shall you walk in their ordinances. You shall observe My judgments and keep My ordinances, to walk in them: I am the LORD your God. You shall therefore keep My statutes and My judgments, which if a man does, he shall live by them: I am the LORD.
–Leviticus 18:1-5

Now it shall come to pass, if you diligently obey the voice of the L*ORD your God, to observe carefully all His commandments which I command you today, that the* L*ORD your God will set you high above all nations of the earth. And all these blessings shall come upon you and overtake you, because you obey the voice of the* L*ORD your God.* –Deuteronomy 28:1-2

Only be strong and very courageous, that you may observe to do according to all the law which Moses My servant commanded you; do not turn from it to the right hand or to the left, that you may prosper wherever you go. This Book of the Law shall not depart from your mouth, but you shall meditate in it day and night, that you may observe to do according to all that is written in it. For then you will make your way prosperous, and then you will have good success. Have I not commanded you? Be strong and of good courage; do not be afraid, nor be dismayed, for the L*ORD your God is with you wherever you go.*
–Joshua 1:7-9

Trust in the L*ORD with all your heart,*
And lean not on your own understanding;
In all your ways acknowledge Him,
And He shall direct your paths.
Do not be wise in your own eyes;
Fear the L*ORD and depart from evil.*
It will be health to your flesh,
And strength to your bones. –Proverbs 3:5-8

When you lie down, you will not be afraid;
Yes, you will lie down and your sleep will be sweet.
–Proverbs 3:24

Like a flitting sparrow, like a flying swallow,
So a curse without cause shall not alight.
–Proverbs 26:2

As you do not know what is the way of the wind,
Or how the bones grow in the womb of her who is with child,
So you do not know the works of God who makes everything.
In the morning sow your seed,
And in the evening do not withhold your hand;

For you do not know which will prosper,
Either this or that,
Or whether both alike will be good.
–Ecclesiastes 11:5-6

"No weapon formed against you shall prosper,
And every tongue which rises against you in judgment
You shall condemn.
This is the heritage of the servants of the LORD,
And their righteousness is from Me,"
Says the LORD. –Isaiah 54:17

He has shown you, O man, what is good;
And what does the LORD *require of you*
But to do justly,
To love mercy,
And to walk humbly with your God? –Micah 6:8
The LORD *is good,*
A stronghold in the day of trouble;
And He knows those who trust in Him.
–Nahum 1:7

Let your light so shine before men, that they may see your good works and glorify your Father in heaven.
–Matthew 5:16

But you are a chosen generation
a royal priesthood, a holy nation,
His own special people, that you may proclaim
the praises of Him who called you out of darkness
into His marvelous light.
-1 Peter 2:9

Additional Resources

Ancient Paths - Craig Hill
Ancient Words - John Waller (music)
Bedtime Blessings, Vol. 1 - Dr. John Trent
The Blessing - Dr. Gary Smalley & John Trent, Ph.D.
TheBlessing.com
The Blessing - John Waller (music)
Blessing Your Spirit - Arthur A. Burk and Sylvia Gunter
Courageous (movie)
Craig Hill on YouTube (http://bit.ly/1ctVtJ8)
Focus on the Family (http://bit.ly/1c4aV3N)
I'd Choose You - John Trent, Ph.D.
The Love Dare - Alex and Stephen Kendrick
The Name Book - Dorothy Astoria
The Power of a Parent's Blessing - Craig Hill
SimplyRebekah's Love Letter Shower
(http://bit.ly/1gyV0fU)

Index A: *Alphabetical by Name*

Index B: *Alphabetical by Character Quality*

About the Author

Christ follower, helpmeet, and momma are the most important titles Kayla Grey claims as her own. Through the ministry of *Family Foundations, International* and Craig Hill's *Ancient Paths* seminars, Kayla's parents learned about the importance of blessing. In 2007, Kayla received her first intentional blessing, and her life hasn't been the same since. Intrigued by the change she witnessed in her parents' marriage, Kayla also attended the seminars, was trained by FFI for ministry, and began to study God's Word in light of what she learned. And from that study over nearly 7 years' time came *Empowering Generations: Blessing from God's Word.*

Kayla is also the author of *Cash Flow Your College: Knowledge in Your Head Without Getting in the Red*, an eBook to equip high school and college students to pursue a degree debt-free. She spends her time laughing with her family, reading, memorizing God's Word, and blogging at Renown and Crowned.
(http://1chron291113.wordpress.com/)

Now to Him who is able to keep you from stumbling,
And to present you faultless
Before the presence of His glory with exceeding joy,
To God our Savior,
Who alone is wise,
Be glory and majesty,
Dominion and power,
Both now and forever.
Amen.
Jude 24-25

Made in the USA
Charleston, SC
17 February 2014